Tikal Report 23A

MISCELLANEOUS INVESTIGATIONS IN CENTRAL TIKAL

University Museum Monograph 114

Tikal Report 23A

MISCELLANEOUS INVESTIGATIONS IN CENTRAL TIKAL

H. Stanley Loten

Series Editors

William A. Haviland
Christopher Jones

UNIVERSITY OF PENNSYLVANIA MUSEUM
of Archaeology and Anthropology
Philadelphia

Library of Congress Cataloging-in-Publication Data

Loten, H. Stanley
Miscellaneous investigations in Central Tikal/ H. Stanley Loten
          p. cm. — (Tikal Report; 23A)
Includes bibliographical references and index.
ISBN 1-931707-39-1 (alk. paper)
1. Tikal Site (Guatemala). 2. Mayas—Antiquities. 3. Mayas—Dwellings. 4. Land
          settlement patterns, Prehistoric—Guatemal—Tikal Site. 5. Excavations
          (Archaeology)—Guatemala.
I. Title. II. Series: Tikal Reports; no. 23A
F1435.1.T5T54 1958 no. 23A
972.81—dc21

                                                                2002009055

Printed in the United States of America on acid-free paper.

Contents

Illustrations

Map

Figures

Tables

Preface

A mong the various types of durable artifacts produced by the ancient Maya, their architecture is particularly impressive. They were prodigious builders, not merely in terms of scale, but also in the sheer number of buildings they erected. Although the Tikal Project excavated many of these and recorded them in detail, and subsequent projects have cleared others, the forests around the site center still hide well-preserved, very ambitious works of native American architecture. Many of these compare favorably with the most celebrated buildings of other world cultures.

Most of the standing architecture is within the inner suburb of the monumental site center, probably serving or housing upper levels of elite society and central institutions of power at Tikal. They were fabricated almost entirely in masonry and many were adorned with elaborately sculptured facades. Tree roots have destroyed most of the surface detail, wooden lintels have rotted, large sections of vaulting have fallen, and bat dung covers many floors. Despite all this collapse, some rooms remain nearly intact. Apart from the accumulation of forest litter and animal leavings, the buildings seem to have been left clean of their former contents. They are now dark, dank, and moldy; when tree cover is removed, however, the rooms become quite habitable.

When it became clear early in the Tikal Project that only a few of these structures would ever be excavated, it was decided to mount a survey to collect the data accessible on the surface. The ensuing architectural survey was not expected to excavate and encounter artifacts other then the buildings, and therefore architects rather than archaeologists seemed appropriate for this assignment. This provided an opportunity for architects, such as Andras Nagy, Hans-Ruedi Hug and myself to work on this survey.

I happily acknowledge the debt I owe to my archaeological colleagues, in particular William R. Coe, who personally supervised my efforts and whose vision guides the Tikal Reports. I feel most fortunate to have been introduced to archaeology by Coe. His is the guiding concept that individual structures should be described in their own terms without reference to others and that primary descriptive data should be kept apart from analytic treatment. The system, in the reports that follow, is Coe's; the lapses are mine.

The American Section of the University of Pennsylvania Museum provided monumental assistance in preparing the manuscript. The late Linton Satterthwaite provided me with office space at the University Museum. Christopher Jones and Carmen Chappel did a very thorough job of editing, and adding references to recent investigations, such as those of Rudi Larios and Miguel Orrego, who later excavated some of the structures that I recorded. Carl Beetz corrected the figures and Jones assembled the figures and plates for this volume. Barbara Hayden computer-processed the manuscript, finished the preparation of the illustrations for publication, and continued the copyediting of the manuscript. Any errors that have survived these numerous filters may be laid at my doorstep. Final stages were guided by Walda Metcalf and Matthew Manieri. I must also thank Jeffrey Quilter and Norman Hammond for reading the manuscript and making very constructive suggestions.

My studies at the University of Pennsylvania were supported by the Canada Council and the Wenner-Gren Foundation. I am very grateful for their assistance.

1

Introduction

Tikal Project investigations in the central area included various programs that were independently conducted at different times by different people. Where such studies have examined diverse aspects of an architectural group, or included an excavation, they are collated as separate Tikal Reports (TR.) or as other parts of TR. 23 (TR. 12:57).

Tikal Report 23A describes groups and structures that were recorded under the architectural survey program, but not examined by any other investigation. It is, therefore, almost exclusively architectural and not excavational in content, and represents only a portion of the recording done under the architectural survey. The structures described (Map 1) are scattered over the entire central Tikal zone and are brought together only by the accident of being bypassed in other studies.

Robert Cooper started the architectural survey in 1963 under the initial guidance of William Coe and Aubrey Trik. Hans-Ruedi Hug and Andras Nagy continued the survey in 1964, and I directed the survey from 1965 to 1969. Miguel Orrego, Rudi Larios, Richard Brown, William Brown, and Payson Sheets assisted in the fieldwork. It was initiated as a surface survey of standing architecture within the boundaries of the Tikal National Park (TR. 12:39–41). From 1963 to 1969, approximately 40 structures were recorded in this program, which included many so-called satellite groups located kilometers distance from the site center and not described here.

Standing architecture, as defined by Carr and Hazard (11:5), is represented by hatching on the site map. Hatching was applied to structures with at least one main building wall standing clear of debris (our survey shows that all were vaulted.) There are approximately 80 (more than 10%) of the mapped structures within the central 16km^2 of the site. More than half occupy groups that underwent excavation and are thus covered in other Tikal Reports. Thirty-five were not excavated, but were recorded in the survey. Fourteen of these also occur in groups that received further study, and are included in other parts of TR. 23. Twenty-one structures are treated in TR. 23A: six individually, and 17 as members of groups.

The goal of the survey was not to record all hatched structures depicted in TR. 11. In selection, the criterion was a visibly identifiable building plan. This restriction resulted in the exclusion of some hatched structures and inclusion of one or two others not thus identified. Some structures were added with visible architectural features but without sufficiently intelligible plans.

The standing structures provide an extensive body of architectural data that are accessible without costly excavation. Because the purpose of the survey was to collect these data, excavation was confined to already visible features that could be significantly clarified by minor clearing or where overlying debris appeared shallow.

After removal of underbrush, the first step in the recording of individual structures was identification of the frontal façade. Stair and doorway positions usually showed this unequivocally; however, in instances of ambiguous orientation, a structure was assumed to face upon the largest adjacent plaza. An axial section/profile was recorded from the highest surviving point to front and rear basal levels, resulting in a debris profile with a few features at the top. Control was by line-level and plumb bob. The profile provides grounds for inferring substructural form and for estimating the volume of building materials (as entered in the time span tables). Because the survey could not determine presence or absence of underlying earlier constructions, these volumes should be regarded as maximal for a given locus.

The plan measurement of the building was also consistent. A method specifically adapted to unexcavated structures was developed, and is worth describing in detail. Tightly stretched, horizontal string-lines were set up around the building at approximately the same level, roughly parallel or perpendicular to each other and as close as possible to each major wall surface. Thus, an irregular network of string-lines was extended around the building and inwards to any doorway or room. The magnetic azimuth of each line was measured to the nearest half degree by Brunton compass on a non-ferrous tripod with elevator and tilting arm. Measurements were then taken along the string-line and from the line to points of interest.

The method is particularly effective for recording irregular or undulating wall lines and for determining confined interiors where transit control is almost impossible to achieve. Brunton readings are not as accurate as transit ones; however, by setting up a complete traverse around the building, a measure of closure can be obtained, and errors can be detected. In general, the anticipated degree of accuracy for a perimeter of approximately 50 m is to the nearest 5 cm or 0.1%, entirely adequate for the recording of building plans. Measurements were registered in notebooks and later translated into scaled drawings.

In most cases, it was possible to gain additional off-section data concerning walls and vaults. Vault fragments often remained standing near the ends of rooms; by cleaning the surface of a fracture, a detailed section can be obtained. Because fractures are often far from vertical, details recorded near the top may be displaced horizontally 1 m or more from those below. Resultant sections, therefore, tend to be composite.

The drafting conventions of TR. 14 and other excavation reports have been followed here, with some exceptions. Because sectional data in unexcavated structures can only be recorded where they happen to be visible, strict adherence to the Tikal standards would require a separate drawing for each bit of data not in the same vertical plane. To avoid proliferation of figures, and for ease of readability, sectional details are placed in axial section/profiles when they describe axial conditions. Details atypical of axial conditions are shown in separate drawings.

Designation of architectural features follows the conventions set forth in TR. 5 and TR. 12, with minor exceptions. For example, because the architectural survey did not engage in deep excavation, developmental designations, such as "1st," "2nd," are not applicable.

The concept of construction stages (TR. 5:9) has been employed as the chief organizing device for architectural description. A construction stage (as the term is used here) is considered to represent a subdivision of a structure that was completed and could stand for a significant time before work started on the next component. These stages can be recognized by the presence of plaster, or substantial mortar surfaces, supporting subsequently installed parts of the structure. Pauses would have allowed for quarrying and assembly of material. Some construction stages (e.g., vaults, as marked by plastered vault-back surfaces) might have been designed to protect against erosion during the necessarily slow work of carved upper-zone installation.

Architectural form is described by a set of visual components (Satterthwaite 1943:15–19). Although these appear to be whole segments of the structure, their reality is often not reflected in construction pauses or plaster floors. Therefore, they may or may not correspond with construction stages.

The visual components of a structure are, from uppermost down: roofcomb; upper story; upper-story building platform; roof structure; upper zone; building walls; building; building platform; supplementary platform; and pyramid. A roofcomb is a feature standing above upper-zone level and lacking accessible interior space. An upper story has accessible interior space (i.e., doorways). If the feature does not have the form of a building or a roofcomb, it is called a roof structure. A platform that sustains an upper story building is an upper-story building platform. Interior platforms are bench-like constructions within rooms. A building has one or more rooms defined by walls and may have vaults and upper zones. The upper zone of a building is the horizontal architectural member that stands above the walls and roughly corresponds in level to the vaults. Most upper zones have two projecting moldings, medial and superior. Specialized medial corbels form the lowermost course of most upper zones. Substructural components are solid platform features that sustain building components. The building platform directly supports a building and usually conforms to it in plan. A pyramid is defined by its form, near-square in plan and high relative to width. A non-pyramidal sustaining component under the building platform is a supplementary platform.

The vertical outer surfaces of platforms, terraces, or walls are called facings, not walls. Walls extend vertically and separate spaces; terraces and platforms extend horizontally and provide horizontal surfaces or floors. The inner masonry of both walls and platforms is the core. Facings are set either as headers (largest dimension into core) or stretchers (largest dimension on the surface). Width, height, and depth (W, H, D) are defined by in situ position, so that width is always the horizontal surface dimension (the term length is not used in tabulation). Facing stones are laid on-edge or flat, and are sharp-cornered or subrectangular (cushion shaped).

Many facings indicate that, after construction, the entire surface was dressed to a smooth flat plane that was then plastered. This procedure is called post-installation dressing.

The inside facing of a vault is called the soffit; the specialized vault stones forming it are either soffit headers or stretchers. Units running the length of the room are the longitudinal or half-vaults; those spanning the short dimension are the end vaults. The outer surface of a vault mass is called the vault-back facing. A timber false-work is a postulated temporary support for beams prior to vault construction.

Each structure report contains an "Architecture" section presenting a summary of attributes for establishment of morphological classification and chronological sequence. In this regard, the terms "early" and "late" are used loosely to indicate the relative chronological placement that is expected to be established through analysis of the complete sample of Tikal architecture TR. 34 (TR. 12:59).

Group 3D-14, Group H

Group 3D-14 (Fig. 1–7) consists of Structure (Str.) 3D-40, at the E end of the Maudslay Causeway and Str. 3D-41, 42, and 43, which share a single platform at the N end of the adjoining Maler Causeway. Together with Gp. 3D-2 Complex P (TR. 18), these structures form the central features of the North Zone (TR. 11). The group was discovered by Edwin Shook in 1937. His map and a brief description were published by Morley (1937–38, I:279, Fig. 14), who named it "Group H." Shook later produced a more complete description with drawings and photographs (1951:12–18, Figs. 1, 20–24).

Although only three of the structures appear on the TR. 11 map as "standing architecture," all four show visible features to varying degrees. Recording of the group was done by Moholy-Nagy in 1964 and by Loten in 1966.

Structure 3D-40

Structure 3D-40 (Figs. 1 and 2) was numbered 93 by Morley (1937–38, I:279, Fig. 14) following its discovery by Shook. Plan, section, and a detailed description are given by Shook (1951:14–15, Fig. 22–24). It has two vaulted rooms on a substructure high enough (approximately 8 m; Shook [ibid., 14] estimates 10 m) to suggest a low pyramid. It stands by itself, facing W at the E edge of a large platform where the Maler and Maudslay Causeways meet. The substructure is almost entirely concealed by rubble. The building itself is nearly intact with the outer half vault fallen only above the front doorway, filling the central part of the two rooms. Back-room vaulting is intact, and upper-zone masonry survives along the rear and sides.

Construction Stages

Stage 4: Building Platform and Substructure

A plastered surface under the exterior walls of the building (Fig. 2) should be the top of a building platform. It is the first evident pause-line in the building process. The surface under the building platform is not known; hence, it and the assumed underlying supplementary platform form a single construction stage.

The supplementary platform is entirely concealed beneath debris. A stair bulge on the W side is visible. Total supplementary platform height should be 6 m. Presence of a building platform is inferred from a horizontal strip of eroded core material immediately below the exterior wall facing, as exposed at several points around the building (Fig. 2). Debris has accumulated to ca. 1 m below the wall. From this evidence, ca. 1.5 m is assumed for the building-platform height.

Stage 3: Building Walls

The walls are identified as a construction stage distinct from that of vaults by the presence of hard, smooth plaster on their tops. Apparently, they were finished and plastered on interior, exterior, and top surfaces before vaulting began. There is no evidence that work actually stopped for any meaningful length of time.

Exterior wall masonry consists of unusually small facing stones (Table 1), rectangular on the face, taper-

Table 1
Structure 3D-40
Facing-Stone Dimensions (m)

	Number	Mean (m)	Standard Deviation	Range (m)
Exterior wall width	100	0.17	4.42	0.08–0.31
Exterior wall height	99	0.07	1.88	0.03–0.15
Interior wall width	25	0.19	5.46	0.10–0.31
Interior wall height	22	0.08	2.17	0.04–0.11
Vault width	40	0.28	2.45	0.21–0.37
Vault height	40	0.28	2.94	0.23–0.37

ing to a narrow, pointed butt and installed as headers. Pieces are trapezoidal in plan, almost triangular, with top and bedding surfaces roughly parallel. Dimensions show a high degree of standardization, with only a few pieces much larger than the average. Blocks were dressed after installation to produce a regular wall face. Mortar joints are thin, and spalls are absent. Exterior wall plaster survives only below the wall top. Interior masonry is essentially identical to the outside, although largely covered by thin white plaster.

Walls vary in thickness from 1.65 m at the front to more than 5 m at the rear. Eight inset end-grooved panels are visible on exterior walls out of a probable total of nine (Fig. 1:4). Small holes, possibly used for scaffolding, are aligned approximately 0.40 m below the wall top (Fig. 1:2). One on the rear wall still has an exterior plaster seal, suggesting use only during construction. Some walls, both interior and exterior, have pronounced batter, whereas others are nearly vertical. In Rm. 2, which occupies a higher level than the front, Fl. 1 abuts primary wall plaster, either as a primary or secondary pavement.

Stage 2: Vaults

A plastered vault-back surface (Fig. 2:1) indicates that the vaults were constructed separately from the roof. There appear to be two such surfaces above both the front room capstones and the front medial molding. The structure could have stood for some time in this incomplete state, its vault masses sealed against water by the two plastered surfaces.

Logically, the initial operation in construction stage (CS.) 2 was installation of wooden lintel beams over the two doorways. Their beds had been previously prepared and plastered along with the wall tops (Fig. 1:3). The lintel over the outer doorway has decayed completely and

seven unmodified logwood beams (0.15 to 0.18 m in diameter) remain over the inner doorway (Fig. 2) of a probably 13. Medial corbel stones were set on the rear wall-top plaster and over a supra-lintel course in the front part of the building. Two courses of supra-lintel masonry are faced by veneer stones, averaging 0.24 by 0.26 m across the front interior wall face. These large blocks are unlike the smaller facing material of the preceding construction stage. There is no evident constructional break between the supra-lintel masonry and the vault.

Vault stones are uniformly coursed headers from 0.40 to 0.60 m deep. Usually the smallest dimension is horizontal, although average values for width and height are both 0.28 m (Table 1). Bedding planes are also horizontal. Blocks taper in plan to a narrow butt, and surfaces were dressed after installation. A coat of thin white plaster covers supra-lintel masonry, feathering out onto wall plaster below. Capstones are preplastered. Round vault beams, averaging 0.15 m in diameter, occur in three levels (Fig. 2).

Stage 1: Roof and Upper Zone

The roof surface is reconstructible from the flat humus layer that extends across the building top. There appears to be a step-up in this expanse between the front and rear. No remains of a roof comb or other construction are visible above the roof.

Upper zones are at three levels: a lower forward part, an intermediate one at the side insets, and a higher rear part. Two mask panels survive on either side of the central doorway area and two at the front corners, but detail has disappeared. Corner masks appear to portray large diagonally facing human heads. A medial molding runs below the sculptured feature in the front (Fig. 2), but the rear has neither a molding nor sculpture. No traces of upper-zone plaster or paint are visible anywhere.

Modifications

Unit 1 in Rm. 1 (Fig. 2) is a horizontal, plastered surface visible near its N end. Either a raised floor or the top of an unusually low interior platform, it abuts primary wall plaster as secondary construction whether built immediately or significantly later.

Other Features

Graffiti are especially abundant on the vertical plaster surfaces of both chambers often incised over earlier ones (TR. 31: Fig. 1–11). They depict human figures, monsters, and pyramidal temples.

Relationship to Adjacent Stratigraphy

Surface contours indicate that Str. 3D-40 stands on a platform commensurate in level with the ends of the Maudslay and Maler Causeways and with Gp. 3D-2 (dated by St. 20 as 9.19.0.0.0). Its temporal relationship to these entities was not determined by excavation.

Table 2
Structure 3D-40: Time Spans

Time Span	Unit and Floor	Comment
1		Abandonment and collapse
2		Use inferred; graffiti?
3	U. 1	Interior platform
4		Use inferred; graffiti?
5		CS. 1-4; ca. 8,600 m^3

Architecture

Structure 3D-40 has a substructure of medium height, two chambers, side insets, rear outsets, a single front doorway, and no roofcomb.

Exterior building form bears little direct relationship to the room arrangement. The three divisions to the upper zone from front to rear do not correspond to the number of chambers. To achieve the three exterior divisions, the front medial moldings are located well below the vault-spring level and the rear ones coincide with the vault-spring and wall top. Despite the fact that the front part of the building is narrower than the rear as seen from the side, the rear room is smaller than the front, and the back of the building is mostly solid masonry. The contrast suggests that exterior form had specific meaning different from that of the room arrangement.

The technical attributes of Str. 3D-40 suggest a late date of construction within the TR. 23A sample (see Chronological Conclusions). These comprise tapered vault headers; wall-facing stones cut to a regular rectangular shape; dressing of masonry surfaces after installation; wall-top plaster; vault-back plaster; preplastered capstones; thin white single-coat interior wall plaster; straight-line profiles on masonry surfaces; equally well finished interior and exterior surfaces; and carving of frontal upper-zone sculptural detail in stone rather than dependence on stucco. A few possibly anachronistic early attributes include the plaster floor under the building walls, diminutive wall-facing stones, and exterior inset panels.

Structure 3D-41

Structure 3D-41 (Fig. 3a–4) is a small, two-room, north-facing building atop a low substructure. It and the identical 3D-42 flank the approach to Str. 3D-43. Morley numbered it Str. 91 (1937–38, I:279, Fig. 14). Shook (1951:14) describes it correctly as having two parallel rooms. The rear wall and half vault are standing. Debris fills both rooms to the vault spring and conceals the exterior of the partly fallen side walls. The front wall does not protrude above the surface. In 1964, Moholy-Nagy made two small excavations: one at the NW corner and the other at the rear center. Apart from these, the structure was recorded by surface inspection.

Construction Stages

Stage 3: Walls and building Platform

No plastered surface intervenes between the walls and the building platform. As a result, these two features constitute an initial stage of construction. Plastered wall tops mark the completion of the stage.

The building platform is simple (Fig. 4). Its full height is unknown because a plaza floor abutting (Plat. 3D-7: Fl. 1; Fig. 4) was probably laid subsequently. Facing stones are large rectangular slabs smoothly dressed after installation. Merely rough-dressed on the face, they were left in place until walls had been com-

Table 3
Structure 3D-41
Facing-Stone Dimensions (m)

	Number	Mean (m)	Standard Deviation	Range (m)
Exterior wall width	100	0.19	5.20	0.10–0.31
Exterior wall height	100	0.10	3.51	0.03–0.21
Interior wall width	18	0.15	3.34	0.12–0.25
Interior wall height	18	0.09	3.06	0.04–0.14
Supra-lintel width	5	0.58	5.46	0.51–0.67
Supra-lintel height	5	0.26	2.68	0.21–0.20
Rear-vault width	40	0.32	6.33	0.21–0.46
Rear-vault height	40	0.30	3.09	0.23–0.36
End-vault width	13	0.32	6.11	0.22–0.45
End-vault height	13	0.31	3.37	0.26–0.36

pleted and both wall and building platform could be facially dressed together. This might explain why wall and building platform batters are similar.

Walls are visible to their full height only at the rear. The outer face consists of small stones (averaging 0.10 to 0.19 m; Table 3), rectangular on the face, horizontally laid, inconsistently coursed and unspecialized as headers or stretchers. Mortar joints are of medium thickness and largely free of spalls. Plaster survives across part of the posterior façade. The interior surface is visible only at the top of the back wall, and is essentially identical in masonry size and shape (Table 3).

Only Rm. 2 could be measured. From the position of the excavated W front outside corner, the side walls are assumed to have outsets as shown in Fig. 3a. Plastered wall tops are on a single level in the front and rear parts of the building.

Stage 2: Vaults

A plastered vault-back surface at the rear of the building (Fig. 4) proves that the vaults were built separately from the roof and upper-zone façade. The rear vault is the only one fully extant and accessible. It rests on a course of supra-lintel masonry of large veneer stones (Table 3), rectangular on the face, laid almost equally flat and upright and consistently coursed. Although course levels extend continuously around the vault, individual stone heights vary considerably. These vault surfaces were also dressed after installation.

Capstones were preplastered on their under surfaces.

There is a plaster coat on the upper face of the capstones as well, probably the horizontal component of the plastered vault back where it extends over the vault masses. Beam holes occur in two levels on the vault face, the upper one at a masonry course level and the lower one midway between course levels (Fig. 4).

Stage 1: Roof and Upper Zone

The actual roof has been lost due to collapse and erosion. At the rear, the upper-zone facing consists of large, rectangular veneer stones dressed after installation. There is no surviving medial molding or rear-sculptured panel.

The rear upper zone extends so high above capstones that a roofcomb or other roof structure is suggested by the profile of surviving masonry. This would have been built at the same time as the upper zone, because there is no sign of an intervening plaster surface.

Relation to Adjacent Stratigraphy

Platform 3D-7: Fl. 1 abuts Str. 3D-41, but might be a platform addition. The building could be contemporary with 3D-42, 3D-43, and the platform that sustains all of them.

Architecture

Although Str. 3D-41 has an extremely low substructure, it is nearly square in plan, and has little interior space. Its two rooms are not wide, it has a rear side outset, and it may have had a roof comb. These are all "temple" attributes. As a temple, it is unusual in being frontally contracted and in lacking a center rear outset.

Technical attributes are nearly all late: no floor under the walls; dimensionally standardized wall-facing stones; specialized tapered vault headers; wall-top plaster; pre-plastered capstones; and masonry surfaces dressed after installation. One early trait is the small size of the wall-facing stones similar to those of Str. 3D-40 and 43.

Table 4
Structure 3D-41: Time Spans

Time Span	Unit and Floor	Comment
1		Abandonment and collapse
2		Use inferred
3		CS. 1-3; ca. 200 m^3

Structure 3D-42

Structure 3D-42 (Fig. 3b) is the western equivalent of 3D-41. It was numbered Str. 92 by Morley (1937-38, I: Fig. 14) and Shook (1951:14). Although less well preserved and more engulfed by debris than 3D-41, it nevertheless presents an item not accessible in the eastern structure: the contraction from rear to front (Fig. 3b). All other aspects of 3D-42 in Fig. 3b are assumed to be equivalent to 3D-41.

Structure 3D-43

The largest individual structure in the North Zone and one of the major architectural entities at Tikal, Str. 3D-43 (Fig. 5-7) is a three-room temple-like building facing S on a large pyramidal substructure. Like 3D-40, it lacks a roof-comb. It was first discovered by Shook (in Morley 1937-38, I:279, Fig. 14), who later published a plan and description (1951: 13-14, Fig. 19-21).

The building itself is almost intact. Vaults and upper zones have fallen over the doorways only. The substructure, on the other hand, has either lost its exposed facing

masonry through erosion or lies hidden beneath debris. Minor modifications are visible within the building, but there is no noticeable evidence of major alterations or additions. Recording was confined to surface inspection.

Construction Stages

Stage 4: Substructure

Completion of the substructure is marked by a hard, plastered surface running under the walls of the building (Fig. 6:1), probably the top of a building platform. Near the base, one can see a stair-side facing of large, well-cut rectangular stones, coursed and smoothly dressed, distinctly unlike the small wall stones of the building. The stair wall documents a fully outset flight on the front of the substructure.

Stage 3: Building Walls

The building walls stand on the plastered top of what is probably the building platform. Wall-top plaster marks an end to wall assembly at three levels stepping up from front to rear. The plaster also dips down beside the doorways to form lintel beds.

Exterior wall facings consist of small stones, horizontally laid, not consistently coursed, and not specially shaped as headers or stretchers (Fig. 7b). Most depths exceed heights. Most stones resemble bricks in facial appearance (average 0.06 by 0.15 m). The majority are triangular, tapering to pointed butts that bond tightly to the core.

Exterior mortar joints are thin to medium and have few spalls. Although interior facings are identical to outer ones, they are largely obscured by plaster. Facial surfaces were dressed after installation, with either pronounced or little batter (Fig. 6).

A single inset panel is axially located in the rear outset (Fig. 5), but no other walls contain them. Two beam holes (perhaps for scaffolding) are visible in the panel.

Table 5
Structure 3D-43
Facing-Stone Dimensions (m)

	Number	Number (m)	Standard Deviation	Range (m)
Exterior wall width	100	0.15	5.10	0.07-0.28
Exterior wall height	100	0.06	2.73	0.02-0.14
Vault stone width	40	0.30	3.76	0.21-0.40
Vault stone height	40	0.29	3.62	0.22-0.40
Vault stone length	30	0.58	5.54	0.49-0.70

Four primary cord holders are aligned in upper and lower pairs to screen off the E half of Rm. 2 (Fig. 7). Their vertical wooden pegs have rotted away, leaving casts or sockets in the mortar.

The three rooms step up from front to rear. Their floors abut the walls and might be resurfacings. Interior plaster consists of two thin coats, the outer one showing coarse brush marks.

Stage 2: Vaulting

Vault work is distinguished from that of the roof by a plastered vault-back surface that turns out onto the tops of the medial moldings. Seen only in the front of the building, it is presumed to extend over the entire vault mass. A horizontal plastered surface visible above the Rm. 1 capstones is probably part of this surface. The vaults rest on the plastered wall top at the rear and on supra-lintel masonry at the front.

The first operation in CS. 2, preparatory to vault construction itself, was the setting of wooden lintels across entries and on beds prepared and plastered during wall construction. All lintels have fallen. Mortar casts of butts above inner doorways indicate squared (zapote?) beams ca. 0.15 m high, eight to each lintel. Over the innermost doorway, the outer beam lay exposed in a recess extending past the butt to the end of the lintel bed. The recess beyond the beam had been finished in smooth plaster flush with it.

A course of supra-lintel facing was installed above the lintels and wall tops. Its interior facings are flat veneer stones (ca. 0.28 by 0.25 by 0.20 m), distinct from the wall facing.

The medial corbel course in the front part of the building corresponds in level to the supra-lintel course and in the rear to the first vault course (Fig. 6). The medial molding in the front is two courses high and placed prior to work on the upper zones. As the medial corbels were set across the front of the building, wooden pegs of a rod row (not illustrated) were placed in the mortar between the stones roughly 0.40 m apart. They angle up diagonally from the turn-out into the core and probably represent wood fittings projecting downward. They extend part way across the front and probably over the central doorway. A second rod row is present at the vault-spring level in the N (rear) side of the Rm. 2 extending approximately 2.80 m on each side of the doorway.

The vaults are six courses high, faced exclusively with headers, which are rectangular on the face, higher than they are wide (0.29 by 0.30 m), consistently coursed and tapering both in plan and section to a narrow butt. Face surfaces were dressed after installation. Mortar joints are thin at the surface and free of spalls. From the soffit to the butt ends, the mortar is of high quality, hard and white. Behind the facing stones, the vault cores consist of flat stones bedded in light gray mortar not quite as hard as the soffit face. Facing course levels extend through the vault cores. A vertical fracture line in the vault mass between Rm. 1 and 2 may indicate that construction proceeded by room units rather than through the double-vault mass as a single unit. Capstones are pre-plastered. The angles of the end vaults are much more acute than those of the longitudinal vaults.

The vault-beam pattern for Rm. 3 appears in Fig. 7a. Socket holes are irregular in shape, implying that the beams were unmodified logwood (as is the surviving beam in Rm. 1). Approximate diameters of 26 holes average 0.12 m (standard deviation or sd = 1.23). Socket depths range from 1.92 m to 0.45 m with the shallowest in the upper level (6 averaging 0.84 m, sd = 21.13) and the deepest in the middle level (6 averaging 1.24 m, sd = 36.26). In the bottom, level 7 sockets average 0.96 m (sd = 15.92). Obviously butt depths were not standardized. The three beam levels do not correspond with course levels in the masonry. This indicates that beams were installed first on a timber false-work, and masonry built up around them (as in Str. 5C-13 and others). Beam patterns in the other two rooms are similar.

Stage 1: Roof and Upper Zones

The present humus level (Fig. 6) can be taken as a rough approximation of the roof surface. There appears to have been a step-up in the roof level somewhere between Rm. 1 and 2. The level contour denotes absence of a roof structure.

Upper zones are in three levels: the lowest at the front, the highest at the rear, and an intermediate level between them in the side insets. The front upper zone contains a large sculptured feature flanking and probably above the doorway. Details have not survived. The rear part has a rectangular mask panel on the central axis (Fig. 6). Rear facings consist of large, rectangular, veneer stones smoothly dressed after installation. There is no medial molding on the rear upper zone. Plaster is visible on the under side of the medial corbels with no traces of paint.

Modifications

Smooth hard floors in Rm. 2 and 3 abut primary wall plaster and are probably resurfacings over primary floors.

A series of secondary beam holes are in the E end of Rm. 3 below the vault spring on both sides of the room (Fig. 7a). The holes are rough and irregular, from 0.10 to 0.15 m in diameter, and from 0.05 to 0.019 m in depth. Ragged scars run almost vertically above the holes on the S side of the room where wooden beams were repeatedly inserted and removed. Hence, the beams appear to have had a temporary function, perhaps to support a shelf.

Other Features

Numerous graffiti decorate the interior wall surfaces, some deeply gouged, others lightly incised (TR. 31: Fig. 11, 12). No pits or signs of burning are detectable.

Relation to Adjacent Stratigraphy

Structure 3D-43 is clearly part of the group comprising 3D-41, 3D-42 and the platform that supports them. From the symmetrical positioning of these structures they may all be contemporary. The group as a whole would appear to be functionally associated with and therefore might be contemporary with Str. 3D-40 and the Maudsley and Maler Causeways.

Table 6
Structure 3D-43: Time Spans

Time Span	Unit and Floor	Comment
1		Abandonment and collapse
2		Use inferred: graffiti
3	Fl. 1	Reflooring in Rm. 2 and 3; subspring beam
4		Use inferred: graffiti?
5		CS. 1–4; ca. 12,700 m^3

Architecture

Structure 3D-43 has the following characteristics: frontally expanding, with side outsets, rear axial outset, three rooms, one front doorway, a high substructure, and no roofcomb. It is, however, distinctly rectangular in plan proportions rather than square.

The exterior plan configuration of the building exhibits relative independence from the interior room arrangement. In particular, the excessively thick wall elements at the ends of the rooms serve no purpose other than to increase the exterior frontal length of the building. Furthermore, as seen from the side (E or W), the frontal division of the building is narrower than the rear part, yet the front room is distinctly wider than the rear room. Finally, while upper zones occupy three levels from front to rear, vaults step up only once. These interior/exterior relationships are similar to those in Str. 3D-40, as are its technical attributes.

3

Structure 3D-38

Northeast of Str. 3D-40 (Fig. 8) and 43 of the North Zone stands a large plaza fronted on its western edge by Str. 3D-38. With the exception of this building, the stonework in the group has almost completely collapsed and none of the other structure were cleared, excavated, or described.

The standing features of Str. 3D-38 consist only of the rear-building wall. The front walls and vaults have collapsed and superficially there is not enough detail visible to permit the preparation of a plan drawing of the building component. Nevertheless, when the ruin was examined in 1969, it was decided to record a section profile. At that time, there did not appear to be any location at which limited excavations might yield significant information.

Construction Stages

Stage 2: Supplementary Platform

The top of this construction stage is marked by a horizontal layer of white mortar ca. 5 cm thick (Fig. 8). Although not a hard plastered floor, it is more than just a levelling surface and thus indicates the completion of the lower substructure as a building stage. No feature of core or facing masonry can be seen. A presumed stair on the E side in front of the doorways is not visible even as a bulge in debris.

Stage 1: Walls and Building Platform

The mortar surface intervening between the walls and the building platform is no more distinct than any

other. Therefore, these two components are included within the same construction stage. No plastered wall-top surface is apparent either. Hence vaults also are placed in this stage.

The top course of the building platform survives across most of the rear (Fig. 8), and probably more survives beneath rubble at the front. Surface dressing appears to have been carried out at the same time as that of the wall, as indicated by the relationship between the surface profile and the setting beds of the masonry. The finished surface is smooth and regular; the mortar joints are thin and free of spalls.

Building platform core masonry consists of small stones, up to 0.15 m high, horizontally bedded in tightly packed dark mortar with no air spaces. The core (Fig. 8) retains impressions of the butt surfaces of a fallen lower course that must have projected beyond the surface of the upper course. In other words, the building platform at the rear evidently had two levels.

Rear exterior wall facings consist of veneer stones about 0.16 m thick, rectangular on the face, evenly coursed, and specialized as headers and stretchers. Headers are almost as numerous as stretchers, but do not form an obvious pattern. Because butt surfaces are cut at an angle, the beds are wider than the tops. This shape is also seen in headers, so evidently these were unspecialized facing stones set with their long dimension projecting into the core. Face dimensions are highly standardized (Table 7). Mortar joints are thin and spalls absent. Surfaces were smoothed or dressed after installation of the entire wall facing. Surface profile is straight and regular with no undulation and very little batter.

A distinctive feature of this wall facing is that in many cases the rectangular face shape has been cut on

Table 7
Structure 3D-38
Exterior Wall Facing-Stone Dimensions (m)

	Number	Mean	Standard Deviation	Range (m)
Half-vaults height	22	0.54	2.33	0.24–0.33
Half-vaults width	22	0.26	2.88	0.20–0.34
End-vaults height	15	0.30	2.96	0.24–0.34
End-vaults width	15	0.24	3.32	0.17–0.28

an angle to the natural bedding planes of the stone, so the bedding runs diagonally to the course-levels of the facing. This might represent inferior quality workmanship. At wall-top level a course of medial corbels projects over the wall face. These rest on a mortar bed rather than on hard wall-top plaster and consequently are considered part of the wall construction. The corbels taper from a maximum width of ca. 0.41 m to relatively narrow butts (Fig.8).

No vault masonry exists in situ, but specialized soffit headers are recognizable in the debris-filled rooms. They are rectangular on the face, about 0.20 by 0.30 m. Their sharply tapered butt shapes suggest that they were set on edge. The amount of detritus is not large enough to indicate the presence of a collapsed roof structure.

Architecture

Structure 3D-38 is a single-story, range-type structure with a vaulted building component. The building may have five rooms of which the end two may be set transversely, projecting forward to establish a "U-" shaped configuration, as suggested by surface contours of debris. The building certainly faces E and probably has multiple front doorways.

The structure has at least three major components of exterior form: a lower substructure (unknown except in approximate height, Fig. 8); a building platform; and a building. The intriguing possibility is that the structure together with its building platform may have been erected in one step.

The two rear levels of the building platform, together with the single-range room pattern, suggest that the lower level may relate to the lateral wings.

Most architectural attributes imply a late date of construction. These are dimensionally standardized veneer wall stones, specialized, tapered vault headers; absence of a floor under the building walls; and dressing of masonry surfaces after stones had been installed. One early anomalous attribute is the absence of a plastered wall top.

Table 8
Structure 3D-38: Time Spans

Time Span	Unit Floor	Comment
1		Abandonment and collapse
2		Use inferred
3		CS. 1–2; ca. 1480 m^3

4

Structure 4D-14

Structure 4D-14 (Fig. 9-13; 61a,b) is the only standing building in the south-facing U-shaped group immediately W of Complex O (TR. 11). Maler mentioned it (1911:49) and mapped it with two N rooms intact (1971: Plan 33). Tozzer and Merwin mapped it as Str. 89 in 1910 and Tozzer shows a plan (1911:129–130; Fig. 46; Pl. 29) that seems to represent the central part of the upper story.

In 1967, this structure was examined by Loten as part of the architectural survey. It is buried under rubble and so badly preserved that the central part of the top story rear wall is the only portion standing clear. Upper-story vault fragments still remain in place. Room 5 of the lower building is accessible from the back and leads to Rm. 2 that is half-filled with debris flowing in from the front chamber. Many upper-story details were clarified through minimal clearing operations. A small excavation was made to floor level in front of U. 9 in Rm. 10 (Fig. 12a). Additional recording took place at debris surfaces.

Construction Stages

Stage 6: Building Walls and Substructure

The plastered wall tops of the building mark the first evident pause in the process of construction. The buried substructure provided no basis for subdividing CS. 6.

Existence of a supplementary platform is based on the assumption that the building platform itself would have been similar to that of the upper story. The building is approximately 3.0 m above courtyard level, leaving roughly 2.4 m for a supplementary platform. Debris contours near the NE corner are suggestive of two terraces,

but alternative single-terrace reconstruction is illustrated in Fig. 10 and 13b. The stairway shown on the E side of the supplementary platform must be there, yet does not show up in debris contours.

A building platform was probably 0.60 m high, with a slight batter projecting ca. 0.10 as in the upper story. Absence of a floor or pause-line between building platform and walls is also based on evidence from the upper story.

The building walls are mostly concealed by debris. Where veneer masonry has fallen away at the center rear (Fig. 61b), the wall core shows impressions of the backs of the facing stones (Fig. 12b). Course levels are recognizable as layers of white mortar alternating with the darker core matrix (Fig. 12b:13). Coursing continued through the wall and probably went around the building, as the building walls were built up course by course.

Exterior facings are approximately 0.18 m deep with well-squared, only slightly turtle-backed butts. Core impressions show no headers in the small area visible. Stretcher heights range from 0.34 to 0.38 m. Widths could not be estimated because the butt impressions were too square to leave division marks. Core masonry consists of medium-sized rubble aggregate in a dark, tight, cohesive, weather-resistant mortar.

The small areas of interior wall face visible are covered with a thin white mortar coat that also extends across the wall top from interior to exterior without step-up (Fig. 12b:10). At the center of the back wall of Rm. 2, the top of a niche could be seen just below vault-spring levels, its sill beneath debris (alternative reconstruction in Fig. 10:11).

The plan shown in Fig. 9a is measured at wall-top level in Rm. 5, 2, and 6. Existence of Rm. 1 is discernible

Table 9
Structure 4D-14
Facing-Stone Dimensions (m)

	Number	Mean	Standard Deviation	Range (m)
Half-vaults height	39	0.30	2.33	0.24–0.33
Half-vaults width	39	0.26	2.88	0.20–0.34
End-vaults height	19	0.30	2.96	0.24–0.34
End-vaults width	19	0.24	3.32	0.17–0.28
End-vaults length	—	0.59	5.44	0.42–0.61
Upper-story vault height	5	0.28	2.79	0.23–0.31
Upper-story vault depth	5	0.54	5.84	0.43–0.59

in the debris contours, yet no first-range features were actually seen. Doorway 5 in the rear wall of Rm. 5 is duplicated in Rm. 6 and in doorways of the first range. The lateral extensions are reconstructed from a very small area of interior wall face in Rm. 4. Frontal projection is estimated from debris profiles; rear projection is only assumed. Because of the depth of detritus in the chambers, no cord holders, scaffolding holes, subspring beam holes, or other wall features are visible.

Stage 5: Vaults of the Building

A timber false-work as the initial CS. 5 operation is inferred from the way that notched soffit masonry fits around vault-beam sockets. The beams must have been placed first and the masonry built up around them, requiring some kind of temporary support until the butt ends could be encased in masonry. Completion of CS. 5 is marked by subroof plaster (U. 4; Fig. 12a) and vault-back masonry. Unit 4 is interpreted as a subroof because it appears above the double vault mass and does not extend over the outer half vault.

Preparation work in CS. 5 includes the setting of wooden lintels over doorways. Lintel beds had been plastered with wall tops as part of wall construction. Doorways 6 and 7 retain intact wooden lintels of unworked logwood beams (Fig. 12b) with their butts encased in mortar even with the surface of the wall. Supra-lintel masonry is absent at Dr. 6, but must have been present over Dr. 5 because the lintel bed there is 0.40 below the wall top.

Vault construction proceeded by course levels that extend through the vault cores (Fig. 12b:6). Facing stones are bedded in excellent quality white mortar that runs a short distance into the core mass at each course level and contrasts with the dark muddy core mortar. The stones are exclusively headers with closely controlled face dimensions (Table 9). Face shapes are rectangular with the greater dimension in the vertical. The lower standard de-

viation for heights probably reflects the construction procedure by course levels. Depths are more variable than face dimensions and the stones are shaped to a sharply tapered butt. Half vaults are identical with end vaults.

Soffits are four-courses high and have an additional variable-height leveling course at the top (Fig. 84, immediately below note 4). Face surfaces had been dressed after placement of masonry to a smooth, regular, straight-line profile with outset springs of 0.06–0.10 m at a constant level coincident with the wall tops. The fact that soffit plaster had been applied prior to installation of preplastered capstones is proven by a plaster-turn at capstone bed level (Fig. 12b:5). The bed itself appears to extend over the vault mass and suggests a minor pause between half-vault construction and capstone installation (Fig. 12b:4). Capstones are preplastered across the middle third of their length with a thin white plaster coat. Once in place, they were covered with a thick layer of core masonry topped by a graded ballast and sealed with thin white plaster (U. 2 and Fig. 12a:4; 12b:2) that presumably extends down over the vault back. An unplastered vault-back facing of coursed masonry is observable on the line of section/profile B-B' (Fig. 12a).

A vault-back facing within the double-vault mass between Rm. 1 and 2 (Fig. 11) indicates that vaulting of the first range preceded that of the second. The difference of only 6 cm in capstone height between these two vaults suggests the absence of step-up in floor levels (Fig. 10).

Presumably CS. 5 includes the installation of medial corbels above the exterior wall faces, as in the upper story, but all are either collapsed or remain concealed beneath debris.

The pattern of vault-beam placement in Rm. 2 is shown in Fig. 13a. The same pattern appears to be present in Rm. 6. It was not possible to see them elsewhere. Surviving beams are of unworked logwood roughly 0.10 m in diameter. Socket depths vary from 0.45 m to one socket that runs entirely through the vault mass.

Table 10
Structure 4D-14: Time Spans

Time Span	Unit and Floor	Comment
1		Abandonment and collapse
2		Use inferred
3	U. 3, 6, 11; Fl. 1	Interior platforms Fl. 1
4		Use inferred
5	U. 1, 2, 4; Fl. 2, 3	CS. 1–6; ca. 3000 m^3

Stage 4: Upper-Story Walls and Building Platform, Roof and Upper Zones of the Building

The basis for the unity of CS. 4 is the absence of building roof plaster (Fig. 12a,b). Unit 4 (Fig. 12a,b) is a hard plaster surface that would be interpreted as a roof and establish an additional construction stage if it were more extensive. It can be seen, however, only near the center of the building, not towards the outer wall. There is clearly no pause between building platform and walls of the upper story. Accordingly, the next major pause after the lower vaulting is marked by the wall-top plaster of the upper story.

All upper-zone material of the building has fallen away so the reconstructed profile shown in Fig. 13b, 10, and 11 is based entirely on conventions. Upper-zone height is probably indicated by the base of eroded upper-story, building-platform masonry (Fig. 12a). The constant level assumed for upper zones and roof in Fig. 10 is based on wall-top levels and vault capstones in the building below.

Although badly eroded in the rear façade (Fig. 12a; 61b), the upper-story building platform survives. Its upper surface is slightly higher than the room floors and it is structurally integrated with upper-story walls. Core masonry (Fig. 12b) includes bedded aggregate grading to small aggregate and subfloor ballast. An exterior profile, as reconstructed on the basis of eroded masonry (Fig. 12a:7), has a shallow top outset and a slight batter.

Upper-story walls survive as low fragments except in Rm. 10, where the rear wall stands intact. Enough remains to outline the plan (Fig. 9b), except for the transverse ends that are presumed similar to those in the building. The N end wall of Rm. 8 is visible, but not its width. The upper-story front is evident only from the debris line (Fig. 11).

Rear exterior wall masonry of the upper story consists of precisely shaped rectangular stones set in regular continuous courses with occasional scattered headers. Mortar joints are thin and spalls infrequent. Surfaces had been dressed to a smooth regular line after placement of masonry. Stretchers are veneer types, approximately 0.20 m thick, 0.60 m long, and from 0.28 to 0.34 m high. Interior surfaces retain a single coat of thin white plaster that extends up and across the wall top. All visible wall surfaces are essentially vertical. Because the accessible area of surviving wall surface is quite small, nothing can be seen of features such as cord holders. Scaffolding holes are visible in the rear (Fig. 61b).

Stage 3: Vaults of the Upper Story

The only remaining fragment of upper-story vaulting is a single remnant near the N end of Rm. 10 (Fig. 12a; 61a). The vaulting stage included the setting of medial corbels over exterior wall faces and ended with application of vault-back plaster. Upper-story vaulting is five courses high with room for a leveling course at the top (now fallen). Soffit stones are all headers, rectangular at the face, with the greater dimension vertical, and sharply tapered towards the butt (Table 9). Heights and depths are slightly less than in the lower building.

The soffit had been dressed after completion of masonry placement. The relationship of the soffit plaster to capstone installation could not be established because of disintegration.

Vault-back facing stones are small and facially undressed. An undulating coat of thin white plaster had been applied over an undercoat of mortar that filled in the irregularities between the stones. Plaster extends horizontally above where the capstones would have been and turns out onto the tops of the medial corbels at the base of the vault.

The small area of surviving vault soffit includes two vault-beam sockets for unmodified round beams (roughly 0.10 m in diameter), not very deeply anchored in the vault mass (only 0.35 m in the one measurable example).

Stage 2: Roof and Upper Zones of the Upper Story

The roof of the upper story is probably the plaster surface identified as U.2 (Fig. 12a), even though there is doubt about the overlying material (see CS. 1). Unit 2 is a hard smooth surface that shows no sigh of weathering. All upper-zone material had completely fallen, and profiles are conventionalized (Fig. 13b, 12a).

Stage 1: Roof Structure on the Upper Story

The final building phase of 4D-14 is represented by U. 1 (Fig. 12a), which overlies the smooth, unweathered surface of U. 2 and thus seems to be a primary component of the structure. Remaining amounts are so small that their nature cannot be determined. Unit 1 extends along the entire length of Rm. 10, above U. 2, but no more than 0.30 high. It might be the upper-story roof, but if so, U. 2 would have to be a subroof. In addition, the debris around Str. 4D-14 seems to exceed that found around other two-story structures with collapsed upper stories. As a result, it is inferred that U. 1 is a remnant of a roof structure. Its form and height are, of course, unknown, and the outline shown in Fig. 11 is no more than a rough estimate of size.

Modifications

The only modifications noted are those in the upper story; comparable features could well exist in the lower building, undetected beneath debris.

Units 6, 7, 8, and 9, interior platforms in the upper story, rest on primary room floors (Fig. 9b) and U. 10 and 11 almost certainly do as well, but were not examined at floor level. All visible benches are similar in form to U. 9 (Fig. 12a). Secondary placement is traceable on the basis of wall plaster abutment and associated resurfacing of floors (i.e., Fl. 1 in Rm. 9, and Fl. 3 in Rm. 10). Nonetheless, all maintain a standard of workmanship comparable to that of the primary structure and thus were probably built not long after the original construction. The cut-stone veneer was smoothly finished after installation and plastered with a single thin white coat.

The latest modification, and the only one aside from interior platforms, is U. 3 (Fig. 12a), which overlies Fl. 3 in Rm. 10. This consists of a line of single, cushion-shaped stones stretching across the axial doorway at the inside wall line, like a rough curbing or sill to keep out water. There is no accumulation of occupational trash either inside or outside U. 3; hence, it is unlikely that it was an edge of a soft-earth living floor. The absence of a primary sill implies that entry of rainwater was not a problem initially, but it could have become one when humus built up on the roof of the building, trees had begun to crowd around, and maintenance declined. Therefore, U. 3 may represent Post-classic occupation.

Relation to Adjacent Stratigraphy

There have been no excavations in the immediate vicinity of Str. 4D-14 and therefore nothing is known of adjacent Stratigraphy. The map (TR. 11) indicates a platform and four other structures (4D-11, 12, 13, and 15) associated with 4D-14, all less well preserved. All of them almost certainly face either W or S and consequently lack what we have found to be a preservationally favorable exposure of a rear wall to the W. Surface configurations suggest (speculatively) that 4D-13, 14 and 15 are contemporary, all sustained on a common group platform, and that 4D-11 and 12 are later additions.

Architecture

As reconstructed in Fig. 13b, Str. 4D-14 has a total of six visual components: the supplementary platform, the building, building platform, the upper story building, its building platform and roof structure. No one component coincides with a construction stage because the points selected for major pauses were based on technical considerations rather than the visual ones. On this basis, the structure demonstrates an integration of building technique and architectural form, each operating in terms of its separate demands without impairing the other.

In the lower building, the axial doorways are centered on the rooms and aligned with a rear niche, while nonaxial doorways (seen only in the rear) are placed off the centers of room spaces and face blank walls. Upper story doorways are centered on room spaces, therefore only the axial doorway is aligned with a lower one.

Front/rear distinction appears in the lower building as a difference in the numbers of front and rear doorways, and a difference in room widths. In the upper story the distinction is visible as an absence of doorways in the W façade.

The rear axial room in the lower building is 11% longer than the nonaxial rooms. A difference of this magnitude seems purposeful. In the upper story the axial room is 17% longer than nonaxial rooms, an even greater difference. The same difference (17%) occurs between the widths of first and second ranges in the lower building.

The presence of doorways in the rear of the edifice raises the possibility of a rear stairway or stairways. However, the amount of debris present seems inadequate to conceal stairways and the doorway placement, with a stretch of blank wall at the center, does not suggest their presence.

Late attributes include lack of connection between visual components and construction stages; absence of a floor running under the walls of the building; veneer-type wall stones; surface dressing of masonry after setting; thin, white plaster in one coat only; preplastered capstones; continuous through-wall course levels; upper zone height similar to wall height; and walls relatively thin in relation to room widths.

5

Group 4E-14, Group F

Named "F" Group by Morley (1937–38, I:277; V: 2: Pl. 188), this assemblage comprises Str. 4E-44/48 and 5E-1 (TR. 11, Great Plaza sheet). Both Maler (1911:47–49, Fig. 7; 1971:49–50, Plan 15, 34) and Tozzer (1911:131, Fig. 47) remark on its impressive, rectangular plaza enclosed by four large range-type structures (Tozzer's Str. 74–77), with the four corners of the plaza left open. It is certainly one of the more coherent and orderly architectural groups at Tikal. When judged by its formal attributes, it appears to have been built as a single, enormous undertaking.

Tozzer included this group in his "northern city," with the three Twin-pyramid complexes just to the N and W. Surface contours, however (see TR. 11), suggest a paved linkage to the S and the Mendez Causeway. Structure 5E-18, 19, 20, and 21 seem to line a frontal plaza leading toward the group, and thus Str. 5E-1, the S structure of the quadrangle, might be the front or entry building. If true, Str. 4E-47, although lower than 5E-1, would be the principal structure, opposite the side of formal entry to the plaza. Structure 4E-45 and 4E-48, both about the same height as 4E-47, are too poorly preserved to be intelligible on the surface.

Surface contours suggest that the structures stand on a group platform about 2 m high, completely obscured by debris. Contours immediately surrounding the group reflect the quadrangular, open-cornered configuration, but it is not known if these were paved or faced with masonry.

Although all four structures are symbolized as "standing" in TR. 11, only 5E-1 and 4E-47 presented sufficient information for recording and inclusion in the present study.

Structure 4E-47

Structure 4E-47 (Fig. 14a; 15–18a; 61c–63 b) was named "The Palace of the Twenty Chambers" by Maler (1911:47–49, Fig. 7; 1971:49–50, Plan 15, 34) because it is the northern one in the quadrangle and the best preserved. His plan is fairly accurate and shows secondary features that are now less clear. Even though vaults have fallen in all rooms except 2 and 9, the wall lines are generally visible and vault fragments still stand at the ends of most rooms. A long expanse of rear wall stands entirely clear of debris (Fig. 61c).

Recording was by Loten in 1966. Excavation cleared the doorway for access to Rm. 9 and to reach floor level in Rm. 2 (Op. 122, 152). Because the W half of the building is not preserved as well, only the E half was actually measured. The rest of the plan (Fig. 14a) was drawn by assuming symmetry and by surface inspection of standing features.

Construction Stages

Stage 4: Supplementary Platform

The top of the supplementary platform is marked by a well-made mortar surface running under the building platform (Fig. 15:9) at a level approximately 1m above the estimated platform floor. It is not a plastered surface, but seems more substantial than just a leveling course. No terrace facings or other surface details can be seen and debris contours do not reveal features such as stairways. The reconstructed stairway in Fig. 18a is conjectural.

Table 11
Structure 4E-47
Facing-Stone Dimensions (m)

	Number	Mean (m)	Standard Deviation	Range (m)
Exterior stretcher width	100	0.50	3.31	0.43–0.67
Exterior stretcher height	100	0.30	2.83	0.19–0.36
Interior stretcher width	10	0.48	5.04	0.37–0.55
Interior stretcher height	10	0.25	3.39	0.17–0.29
Interior header width	4	0.20	2.17	0.17–0.23
Interior header height	4	0.28	3.00	0.23–0.31
Half-vault width	40	0.25	2.20	0.21–0.31
Half-vault height	40	0.30	2.51	0.24–0.34
End-vault width	40	0.25	2.34	0.20–0.31
End-vault height	40	0.30	2.52	0.21–0.34

Stage 3: Walls and Building Platform

The walls of the building and the building platform that sustains them are included together in CS. 3 because they appear to have been built as a single operation, its completion marked by the plastered wall tops.

The surface at the top of the building platform is a rough mortar layer more substantial in some places than in others. It appears to have been laid down in sections including both building platform and wall construction.

The only visible building-platform material is a strip of core masonry exposed immediately below the exterior rear wall facing (Fig. 15; 17b; 61d; 63b). Low values of standard deviation in Table 11 indicate high dimensional standardization. Headers occur roughly one to every five stretchers but in no obvious bonding pattern. Surfaces had been dressed to a smooth straight-line profile, generally with no batter, after installation of stones. Mortar joints are thin and spalls absent. Interior facings are essentially identical.

Although plaster has disappeared from exposed exterior surfaces, a thin white coat remains over most of the interior except where the vaults stand over Rm. 2 and 9. There is no evidence of paint on wall surfaces.

Wall cores consist of soft white limestone scraps, not bedded, in dark gray mortar. Course levels extend through the core from interior to exterior surfaces. At each course level, a thin layer of the white mortar in which facing stones are set extends into the core, at times all the way through. This indicates that wall construction proceeded course by course over large parts of the building, possibly over the whole.

Transverse doorways 9 and 11 (Figs. 14a; 16; 17a; 62c) are spanned by masonry vaults with outset springs, flat capstones, and a vault beam. Six openings, identified as "windows" (Fig. 14a; 15; 16b; 17c; 18a; 62b,d) have stone lintels and are square or rectangular with rounded corners and plastered sill and jamb surfaces. Two scaffolding holes (Fig. 16b:7, 9) pass through the rear exterior wall.

The walls define a total of 14 rooms of which 4 are in the lateral side extensions (Fig. 14a). Primary Fl. 2 (Fig. 15; 16b) in Rm. 2 and 9 is a thin (1 cm) plaster topping laid directly on the core masonry with no subfloor or ballast layer. It unites with primary wall plaster and is noticeably smooth and unmarked under the Rm. 9 bench.

Stage 2: Vaults

Vaults rest on the plastered wall tops and are marked as a construction stage separate from that of the roof by an unplastered masonry vault-back surface. The initial operation after completion of the walls preparatory to vault construction was the installation of wooden lintels over all doorways except the vaulted transverse Dr. 9 and 11. Only two lintels even partially survive. The one over Dr. 15 consists of 12 to 15 uncarved logwood beams 0.10 to 0.15 m in diameter. Beam impressions are visible on the plastered lintel bed of Dr. 2.

A layer of supra-lintel masonry was placed on top of the lintel beams as a filler up to the wall-top level. Above Dr. 2, there is no apparent constructional break between supra-lintel and vault material.

Vaulting was started by setting outset vault-spring stones and medial corbel stones on the inner and outer sides of the wall top. These form a base course from which vaulting proceeded course by course. A vault-back facing comes down onto the butt ends of the medial corbels that taper in plan from 0.30 m at the face to 0.15 m at the butt.

Surviving vaults are seven courses high, including a "small course at the top to establish a level bedding for capstones." Vaults are faced exclusively with consistently coursed headers, rectangular on the face (0.25 by 0.30 m), with the greater dimension in the vertical. The stones taper from face to butt in both plan and section, and extend approximately 0.60 m into the vault core. Face surfaces were dressed after installation.

End vaults include both headers and stretchers (Fig. 17b; 63a) and have thinner cores than half vaults. These features suggest that the builders thought of the half vaults as the primary structural members and the end vaults as enclosing units.

Vault-back masonry on half-vault units is coursed, but roughly shaped and minimally dressed on the face. Stones are flat slabs, 0.10 to 0.15 m high, and 0.20 to 0.30 m deep. End vaults have vault-back facings of much smaller stones (Fig. 17b), and are not shaped, coursed, or dressed. There are no traces of plaster on either vault-back or soffit surfaces. Capstones are preplastered on the central strip exposed between the two soffits.

The vertical joints visible between vault units imply that rooms were vaulted by separate crews working simultaneously. Vault beams in Rm. 9 (Fig. 16b) are installed in two levels with doubled beams in the lower level. Vault-beam patterns are also visible in Rm. 2. Sockets in Rm. 9 suggest round beams 0.09 to 0.15 m in diameter; depths vary from 0.28 to 0.65 m in no obvious pattern.

Stage 1: Roof and Upper Zone

The roof has fallen everywhere except over Rm. 2 and 9. Upper-zone fragments survive adjacent to these rooms and at Rm. 15. There is no visible plastered roof surface, but the horizontal humus layer above the two surviving vaults indicates the approximate roof level (Fig. 15).

Upper-zone material at Rm. 15 (Figs. 17b; 61c, d) retains veneer facing stones 0.12 to 0.14 m thick, dressed on all surfaces, and carved after installation. Carving includes fragments of low relief sculpture not sufficient to show motif. The carved panel is recessed 2 cm above the medial molding. No paint or plaster survives.

Upper-zone core material, as found in the single sample examined (Fig. 17b), is made up of medium to small aggregate, not bedded, in a matrix of light gray mortar indistinguishable from that used at the facing. There is no sign of course levels in the upper-zone core.

Modifications

Doorway 9 is partially blocked by Unit 1 (Figs. 14b, 16b), a masonry feature approximately 0.60 m high that filled the lower part of the doorway. Its two vertical surfaces are flush with the primary wall faces and are made of cut-stone masonry and plaster similar to primary wall construction. There is no surviving top surface, but the doorway jamb surfaces above it show no signs of greater height.

Unit 4, a bench in Rm. 9 (Figs. 14b; 15; 16b), abuts primary wall plaster and rests on the primary room floor. The vertical front face has masonry and plaster similar to primary features and U.1. The top is plastered but undulating. Floor 1 overlies the primary floor and joins with U. 4 plaster. It is 1 cm thick, hard, and smoothly finished.

Unit 3 is a comparable bench in Rm. 2 (Figs. 14; 15) and also joins with Fl. 1. Masonry and plaster do not differ from that of primary construction. It has raised ends and a noticeably sloping top surface.

Vault-beam sockets 2 and 5 in Rm. 9 (Fig. 16b) are plugged with chunks of stone. Socket 6 has a plug finished with smooth, hard plaster, the only plaster remaining on the vault soffit. Presumably these features represent primary beams that were later eliminated.

A shallow hole about 6 cm deep has been crudely gouged into the wall surface above U. 4 in Rm. 9 (Fig. 16b:8), probably for insertion of a secondary subspring beam.

On the front of the building adjacent to the S jamb of Dr. 15 are vertically aligned marks and holes that appear to represent a secondary masonry wall no longer standing above the debris level (Fig. 14b: U. 2). The wall was seen by Maler, but is now engulfed by debris. Because there is no obvious concentration of rubble, it cannot represent much masonry. It may have been a screen wall beside the doorway or have supported a thatch roof.

Relation to Adjacent Stratigraphy

The four structures of the group, 5E-1, 4E-45, 4E-47, and 4E-48, occupy a common sustaining platform and adjacent contours imply that extensive grading operations accompanied this construction. In other words, all surface features immediately adjacent to 4E-47 (with the possible excepton of the interior Str. 4E-46) may represent the same event: the construction of the Gp. 4E-14 quadrangle as a unit.

Table 12
Structure 4E-47: Time Spans

Time Span	Unit and Floor	Comment
1		Collapse
2		Use inferred
3	U. 1–4; Fl. 1	Interior platforms subspring beam
4		Use inferred
5	Fl. 2	CS. 1–4; ca. 3000 m^3

Architecture

Structure 4E-47 is pre-eminent in Gp. 4E-14 since it is situated opposite the elaborate portal Str. 5E-1. This may explain the presence of two components (building platform and supplementary platform) on a relatively low substructure.

The building platform is higher at the rear than at the front and there is a corresponding step-up in room floor levels. In contrast, the medial corbels maintain constant level from front to back. A convenient way to resolve the two levels would be to carry the higher one around the lateral side extension to the front, as suggested in the plan (Fig. 14a). This would keep the five front rooms closer to the plaza floor and provide them with higher walls because of the single upper-zone level. The U-shaped plan configuration also distinguishes the front rooms visually by means of the projeting ends. The visual importance of the front-rear axis is further expressed by the greater width of the axial doorway and by the progressively decreasing spaces between the doorways that flank it in the façade.

The two central rooms are the longest in the building and are flanked by short side rooms that must have served some special function. Interior doorways permit circulation through this central suite of six rooms, but not beyond it. The other rooms are each accessible only from the exterior, either in pairs or singly. The placement of Dr. 15 (and 5?) to provide access into the lateral side extension without passing through the S range emphasizes the special nature of these S rooms.

Architectural attributes that indicate late construction include absence of a plastered floor under the walls of the building; presence of plastered wall tops and preplastered capstones; presence of a vault-back surface; veneer wall-facing stones specialized as headers and stretchers on both interior and exterior surfaces; continuity of course levels through walls and around the building; smooth dressing of masonry after

installation; specialized vault-stone shape; and thin white wall plaster. The use of stretchers in the end vaults links Str. 4E-47 with others, possibly of the same time period and even the same builder.

Structure 5E-1

This structure (Fig. 14b; 19; 63c–64b) stands on the S side of the Gp. 4E-14 quadrangle. Maler (1911:48; 1971: Plan 34) mentions the possible presence of plaza-level rooms in its substructure, which is correct, whereas Tozzer, labeling it Structure 74, shows an incorrect "H"-shaped plan (1911:131, Fig. 47). It is much higher than the other three structures that form the quadrangle and, unlike them, appears to have a broad stair on its external side.

Recording was done by Loten in 1966. This included Op. 122A and 152A, both clearing debris to floor level in Rm. 9. All other recording was at debris-surface level. Vaults are fallen but the ends of several remain standing except for Rm. 9. Consequently rooms are filled to wall-top level with rubble. The W half of the building is not as well defined as the E half and was drawn (Fig. 14b) on the assumption of symmetry except where debris contours indicated otherwise.

Construction Stages

Stage 4: Supplementary Platform and Room 11

Completion of the supplementary platform is marked by a hard, plastered surface (Fig. 19:10) that runs under the building platform, approximately 4.5 m above the estimated level of the plaza to the N. On the S side, at the line of Section/profile A-A' (Fig. 19), masonry at debris level appears to be eroded terracing rather than core material.

On the other side of the supplementary platform, in the same line, the walls and vaults of Rm. 11 emerge partially from debris (Fig. 18b; 63d). Pause-lines such as wall tops and vault backs are not present to distinguish construction stages. Room 11, therefore, is included as a part of the supplementary platform.

Wall stones are veneer slabs similar to those in the building walls. Vault headers are larger and less tapered than those in the building, however. Masonry surfaces were dressed after installation of stones; no plaster survives. The rooms are similar to those of the building above in width, but are only about two-thirds as high.

Debris contours suggest that rooms similar to Rm. 11 exist at the substructural base level across the N façade and around the E end, but not at this height on the S façade (Fig. 19). There is a great deal of rubble on the S, however, and rooms at a slightly lower level might open onto the plaza to the S. The lines of outset stairways are clear on the N and S sides of the substructure; that on the S is much wider.

Stage 3: Walls and Building Platform

No plaster floor runs under the walls of the building; therefore, walls and building platform are included together in a single stage of construction. Completion of the stage is marked by the presence of hard wall-top plaster.

The building platform appears on the exterior as a basal molding. Where facings can be seen, they consist of a single course of headers. Face dressing was probably done at the same time that wall surfaces were dressed. No plaster survives.

Walls were constructed in even course levels that incorporate both interior and exterior facings and extend around the entire building. Either course levels were very carefully controlled, or the walls were built course by course. Presence of thin white mortar lenses running into the wall core at course levels imply the latter (Fig. 19).

Exterior wall facings are veneer headers and stretchers (Fig. 63c). Tighter control is evident in heights than on widths (Table 13). Infrequent and randomly distributed headers are identical to stretchers in size and shape; evidently, a standard block was quarried for both. Facing stones were roughly squared to a rectangular shape prior to setting. Afterward, the wall surfaces were dressed to a smooth profile. Interior faces are mostly plaster covered and appear identical with those on the outside.

Facing stones are set in a good quality, hard, white mortar. In contrast, the core masonry is set in dark gray, tight mortar with small aggregate of soft stone scraps. Larger core blocks are cushion-shaped, of the same soft stone used for facings.

Walls are finished with a single coat of hard, thin, smooth, white plaster that extends across the wall top and (originally) down both interior and exterior faces. There is no evidence of paint. In Rm. 9, there are two layers of wall-top plaster, both equally hard and smooth (U. 1 and 2; Fig. 19). The wall top here is possibly either locally settled or initially irregular and repaired prior to vaulting. Elsewhere in the building there is only one wall-top surface.

Because of the depth of debris, interior wall features such as cord holders and subspring beam holes were not observed.

The primary floor in Rm. 9, Fl. 2, has a hard, smooth finish and turns up to wall masonry. It overlies a ballast about 5 cm thick.

Stage 2: Vaults

Vaulting of the rooms in the upper building (in contrast to that in Rm. 11) is definable as a separate construction stage by the presence of both wall-top plaster and vault-back facings (Fig. 19). The initial operation was the installation of wooden lintels over doorway openings. No beams survive, but their presence is attested by the plastered lintel beds that had been prepared as part of wall construction. There is no specialized supra-lintel course of masonry.

Surviving vault springs are at wall-top level. End vault and half vault soffits are similar. Capstone undersurfaces are flat and preplastered. Vault-back surfaces are faced with roughly squared stones, much smaller than wall-facing stones and irregularly coursed. No vault-back plaster can be seen.

Vault-facing stones are tapered into core masonry (Fig. 63d; 64a) and are set in sloping beds. The finished soffit face must have been cut into the surface after the stones had been set in place. From the keying of headers at corners, it is evident that the end vault and longitudinal vault units were carried up simultaneously in course levels that carry through the vault mass (Fig. 19).

Table 13
Structure 5E-1
Facing-Stone Dimensions (m)

	Number	Number (m)	Standard Deviation	Range (m)
Exterior wall width	70	0.50	6.03	0.41–0.58
Exterior wall height	—	0.32	1.92	—
Vault stone width	—	0.25	3.11	0.20–0.32
Vault stone height	—	0.56	5.85	0.48–0.64

As in the walls, vault-stone heights are more precisely controlled than are other dimensions (Table 13).
Most header faces are approximately square.

Stage 1: Roof and Upper Zone

Very little upper-zone material survives. The fragment remaining in the S façade (Fig. 19:4) indicates
that the medial corbels had been installed as part of the
upper-zone construction rather than as part of vaulting. Above the molding a few upper-zone facing stones
indicate the presence of sculptured detail (Fig. 19;
63c), with no trace of plaster or paint.

The flat humus level above the vault mass (Fig. 19)
probably approximates the original roof level that almost certainly did not sustain a roof structure.

Modifications

In Rm. 9, Fl. 1 is a resurfacing over primary Fl. 2 and
under the U. 3 bench. It is only 2-cm thick, soft, and has no
surviving plaster surface where exposed in front of U. 3.

Unit 3 is an interior platform that nearly fills Rm. 9;
it abuts primary wall plaster and lies on top of Fl. 1 and
2. Its facing stones are smoothly finished veneer slabs
slightly larger than those of primary wall facings. No
plaster survives.

Other Features

Excavation in Rm. 9 revealed a deposit representing
occupation prior to major structural collapse, but subsequent to plaster erosion (Lots 122A/1,4; 152A/1,2).
The accumulated material in front of U. 3 and in the
doorway includes probable Eznab pottery, animal
bone, plant remains, charcoal, and fine-grained ash.
Collapse debris seals the deposit.

A remarkable graffito (Fig. 64b; not included in TR. 31)
has been incised in the W end wall of Rm. 9. It does not
appear to represent ancient Maya iconography, but might
document relatively recent non-occupational activity.

Architecture

Structure 5E-1 is a range-type building without lateral side extensions, with doorway openings in both
principal facades, aligned doorways that provide

Table 14
Structure 5E-1: Time Spans

Time Span	Unit Floor	Comment
1		Collapse
2		Use inferred; lots 122A/1-2
3	U. 3	Interior platform in Rm. 9
4		Use inferred
5	Fl. 1	Reflooring in Rm. 9
6		Use inferred
7	U. 1, 2; Fl. 2	CS. 1-4; ca. 5400 m³

through-passage on the axis, and no upper story or roof
structure. It has a relatively high substructure (approximately as high as the building), stairways on both
sides, and vaulted rooms at substructure level.

The two principal facades of the building appear to
be identical in form; neither can be identified as the
front. The substructure has a wider stairway on the S
and rooms on the N, and within the building, rooms are
wider in the S range, possibly indicating that this side is
frontal. It may be that the S façade is the front for the
group and the N is the front of the building itself.

The presence of stairways in both facades, the
through-axial circulation, and the ambiguous frontality
may express a function as a portal structure for entry to
the group. Other aspects of function may be indicated by
the fact that most rooms are accessible individually from
the exterior only. The exception occurs in Rm. 4 and 5,
which are linked and provide an alternative non-direct
pathway of through circulation (Fig. 14b).

Axial rooms are longer than the adjacent rooms that
in turn are longer than end rooms. Doorway widths, as estimated from debris contours, appear to follow the same
pattern. The spaces between doorways therefore auto-
matically diminish outward from the axis.

Attributes that imply a late chronological position
within the present sample consist of a low, minimal building platform; smoothly finished veneer masonry on both
interior and exterior wall surfaces; thin, white plaster in
one coat only; relatively thick walls; plastered wall tops;
absence of a floor running under the walls of the building; preplastered capstones; masonry surfaces dressed after the setting; and incised upper-zone sculpture.

6

Structure 5C-9

One of the largest range-type buildings at Tikal, Str. 5C-9 (Fig. 20–21) has never been cleared and is rarely visited despite its proximity to the road from the Great Plaza to Temple IV. It stands in thick forest immediately N of the Tozzer Causeway and on the E bank of the wide breach that severs the causeway, apparently for the purpose of directing rainwater run-off into the Causeway Reservoir. The structure is in an advanced state of collapse, its rooms entirely filled with vault rubble, its only visible masonry the rear exterior wall. There did not appear to be any location at which limited excavations might produce useful data. A very small hole was opened through debris to the top of the interior wall face in order to provide a wall thickness measurement. Apart from this and the extant rear wall face, all plan data were estimated from debris profiles.

The structure has been described by Maler (1911:40–41; 1971: Plan 35) as "The Sacerdotal Palace Belonging to Great Temple IV." Maler evidently saw 5C-9 as two-storied, although the evidence for this was not visible in 1966. He may have interpreted the lower terraces as a first story or may have seen walls that have since been buried. Tozzer mapped the entity (1911: Pl. 29) as his Str. 73 but made no comments on its configuration.

Because of the poor preservation and the resultant low level of precision in plan measurement, the structure was considered as a marginal candidate for inclusion in the architecture survey. Fortunately, a large portion of the back wall had split in half longitudinally, exposing a long stretch of wall core. Few structures present this pattern of collapse and the masonry characteristics (outlined below) reveal an aspect of the construction process that is not demonstrable in better-preserved buildings, hence the decision to include it in the survey.

Construction Stages

Stage 4: Substructure

Floor 2 (Fig. 21) marks a pause in building at the completion of the substructure and thus distinguishes it as a construction stage. Floor 2 is composed of a white plaster topping, not particularly hard, on roughly 8 cm of fine-grained floor body. Core masonry below includes large dressed stones approximately 0.50 by 0.30 by 0.10 m bedded in a matrix of dark muddy mortar containing medium-sized aggregate (0.10–0.20 m maximum). No facing masonry is visible. A stair bulge approximately 22-m wide can be seen on the W side. Rubble obscures all other details.

Stage 3: Walls and Building Platform

Lack of a floor between the building platform and walls indicates that the two components belong to a single construction stage completed by a hard, smooth plaster surface on top of the exterior rear wall.

The building platform is visible as a horizontal band of core material immediately beneath the foot of the exterior rear wall face (Fig. 21). It consists of unbedded medium to small aggregate. No building-platform facing masonry can be seen, although some may survive beneath debris at the front.

The back wall of the building stands on a rough unplastered mortar level that marks the top of the building platform. Exterior facing stones are rectangular and consistently coursed, although course heights vary considerably (Table 15). The wall is unusually thick (ca. 2.80 m).

Table 15
Structure 5C-9
Exterior Wall Masonry (m)

	Number	Mean (m)	Standard Deviation	Range (m)
Width	35	0.51	3.83	0.40–0.56
Height	35	0.30	5.49	0.21–0.35

For about two-thirds of its length, the exterior facing and part of the core has fallen and eroded away. In the core material thus exposed near the center of the wall, a series of task units, each roughly wide, are observable (Fig. 20:1) through changes in the dark brown color of the mortar matrix. Core masonry consists of horizontally bedded medium to large blocks, some of the larger (ca. 0.50 maximum) shaped like facing stones.

The arrangement of rooms and doorways is recognizable as ridges and valleys in the debris, but no interior facings are visible. One small area of interior wall face exposed by excavation retains a single coat of thin white plaster. Floor 1, presumably the primary room floor (Fig. 21), is noticeable at one end.

Stage 2: Vaulting

A quantity of core masonry stands above the rear wall. All vault facing has fallen and no vault back remains. The vault core consists of medium-sized blocks, horizontally bedded in a tight matrix of light gray mortar.

Stage 1: Roof and Upper Zones

All roof and upper-zone features have disappeared through collapse and are inferred from the presence of vaults.

Relation to Adjacent Stratigraphy

There have been no excavations in this part of the site. Stratigraphic controls are not available. Surface contours (see TR. 11, Temple IV Quadrangle) suggest that the platform sustaining Str. 5C-9 may be part of the Tozzer Causeway.

Architecture

As distinguished by debris contours, the building plan is rectangular with no outsets or transverse ends. There is a single range of three rooms with the central one decisively longer than the other two and containing three doorways. The doorway openings cluster around the central axis, rather than following an evenly spaced pattern from end to end.

The rear height of the building platform implies that it had no front-to-rear step-up. The stairway width appears to correspond to the length of the central chamber. Ground level is higher in the back than in front.

Task lines visible in the posterior wall suggest that portions of wall were built separately, perhaps by different work crews drawing on a common stockpile for larger masonry units. By mixing mortar and small aggregate independently, and working simultaneously, they reduced the time required for construction.

Attributes suggesting late construction include plastered wall tops and absence of a floor under the building walls.

Table 16
Structure 5C-9: Time Spans

Time Span	Unit and Floor	Comment
1		Abandonment and collapse
2		Use inferred
3	Fl. 1, 2	CS. 1–4; ca. 5500 m^3

7

Structure 5C-13

Structure 5C-13 (Fig. 23-29; 64c-65c) has become the "Bat Palace" (in reference to the layer of bat dung that constitutes the only debris in many fully intact rooms) and the "Palace of the Windows" (for the four openings in its rear wall). Well preserved, this range-type structure is two stories high, has five doorways in the front, is raised on a high supplementary platform and faces E. An extensive group platform supports it and two other low structures (5C-11, 5C-12) that form a quadrangular space open to the E. The whole tightly organized group occupies the S side of the Tozzer Causeway between Great Temples III and IV, obviously an important "inner-Tikal" location.

The structure was first recorded by Maler in 1895 as "The Palace of Two Stories with 14+7 Chambers in the Rear of Great Temple III" (1911:38–40, Fig. 6; 1971:48, Plan 24, 35). Tozzer numbered it Str. 69 (1911: Pl. 29). Maler's plan is accurate for the building, but less so for the upper story which he shows as fully preserved—a condition that seems unlikely unless collapse since Maler's time has been severe. He mentions corner masks in the upper zones of which one possible fragment remains.

Recording was done by Loten in 1966. The survey did not include excavation except for minor cleaning of features.

During the 1970s, the building and what remains of the upper story were cleared and consolidated by IDAEH de Guatemala under R. Larios and M. Orrego. Revealed in this operation was a stairway in the E façade providing access to the upper story. It is probable that other features such as benches and cord holders were uncovered, but these are also not included in the present report.

Construction Stages

Stage 6A: Supplementary Platform

A horizontal mortar surface running under the building platform (Fig. 25:11) indicates the top surface of the supplementary platform, approximately 2.30 m above plaza level. This seems to be more than just a bedding level; however, because it is unplastered, it is probably not a finished pause in construction.

Detritus conceals all terrace facings except for one small exposure near the NE corner. Here, facing stones are fully coursed, rectangular on the face, approximately 0.20 m high, and dressed to a smooth, straight-line profile after placement. Batter of 0.06 m in 1.00 m of height may indicate outward displacement due to tree-root action. No moldings were observed in the small part visible and no plaster had survived.

Debris profiles hint that the platform plan follows the outsets of the building (Fig. 23b). A stairway stands on the E side. Considerably longer than the building, the platform extends N to form a wide surface in front of the N doorway. The corresponding area at the S is more deeply buried in rubble and has been inferred from the N end.

Stage 6B: Building Walls and Building Platform

The surface sustaining the building walls appears beneath the primary room floor (Fig. 25:10) as an unplastered subfloor without a mortar topping. At the ex-

Table 17
Structure 5C-13
Facing-Stone Dimensions (m)

	Number	Number (m)	Standard Deviation	Range (m)
Exterior wall width	100	0.53	4.91	0.43–0.65
Exterior wall height	100	0.30	2.99	0.21–0.36
Exterior wall depth	—	—	—	0.13–0.20
Interior wall width	11	0.55	13.5	0.29–0.85
Interior wall height	11	0.29	7.02	0.10–0.38
Half-vault width	40	0.28	2.61	0.23–0.33
Half-vault height	40	0.28	2.22	0.19–0.32
Half-vault depth	7	0.54	6.46	0.44–0.61
End-vault width	40	0.26	2.52	0.19–0.31
End-vault height	40	0.26	2.52	0.22–0.33

terior front the bedding level at the base of the wall is no different from the joints at each course level in the wall. Thus, the building platform was constructed as an integral part of the walls.

The building platform rests on the sloping top surface of the supplementary platform and its exterior top level is also about 0.24 m lower at the rear than at the front. At the same time, there is a step-up in room floor levels from front to rear so that the floor of the rear chamber is about 0.60 m higher than the rear of the building platform.

A small area of facing masonry was observed at the front of the building platform (fig. 25. It is two courses high (ca. 0.80 m), has a slight batter, and projects 0.10 m from the wall face. At the rear, the facing has eroded away entirely, exposing core masonry of horizontally bedded cushion-shaped blocks set in good quality mortar.

The front platform height of 0.80 m would require at least one stair step for entry into the rooms, but whether this consisted of a series of separate units or a single common step is not known. No steps are shown in the drawings.

The building walls are topped by hard, smooth, wall-top plaster. At this point, the builders apparently were concerned about establishing a true level for the subsequent vaulting. They compensated for the downward slope from front to rear of the supplementary platform and also corrected for a low spot around Rm. 3 by adding a second plaster coat to bring the level up about 5 cm. Wall-top plaster drops down on each side of door jambs to form lintel beds (Fig. 25:9). Completion of this stage probably included plastering of vertical wall surfaces, room floors, building platform, and supplementary platform.

Exterior wall facings, with approximately one header to three stretchers, are rectangular on the face, fully coursed, and facially dressed after placement. Low values for standard deviation (Table 17) indicate controlled dimensions with a preferred value near the mean. Depths range from 0.13 to 0.20 m for stretchers. Headers are similar to stretchers in length but are roughly reduced to a tapered butt (Fig. 25 and 65c). Interior facings are similar; these, however, could not be as fully sampled because of plaster cover. Higher values for standard deviation partly reflect the smaller sample size, but also indicate greater variability. Interior head/stretcher frequency is again about 1:3 and surfaces were dressed after placement. No exterior plaster has survived, although the interiors retain a single thin white coat. Core data were not available.

In the rear wall are four windows (Fig. 23; 64d) similar to the one shown in Fig. 26a. All have lintels of unworked logwood beams installed during wall construction. In the primary jamb plaster of each window there is a shallow vertical groove that continues horizontally across the plastered sill (Fig. 26:1). These grooves perhaps signify that the windows had a kind of wooden frame to regulate the passage of wind, water, insects or light. Sill heights are approximately 1.30 m above floor level, that is, close to standing-eye level.

An opening of similar form (ca. 0.45 m square) passes through the E wall of Rm. 11 (Fig. 23b:4). This is at standing-eye level and had plastered jamb and sill surfaces, but is spanned by stones units.

Smaller openings that are spanned by stone, approximately 0.18 m square, pass through the exterior front wall in Rm. 1 and 2. Without plastered jamb surfaces, and placed below eye level, they are probably either small vents or large scaffolding holes made larger than normal in order to facilitate removal of beams after construction. They are neither at the normal scaffolding wall-foot level, however, nor in vertical pairs. Similar holes may exist in the front walls of other rooms, concealed beneath debris.

Ten primary cord holders are located in pairs at Dr. 7, 2, 17, 15, and 16. All have sockets for vertical wooden pegs and circular scars where ceramic inserts had been removed.

Four holes in the back wall of Rm. 8 occur in vertical pairs (Fig. 29b, holes 1–4). The upper holes retain impressions of wooden beams that were installed during wall construction and project into the room, but not all the way across. They might have been scaffolding beams, but their position below vault-beam holes suggests an alternative interpretation as anchorage beams for timber false-work. Further evidence for false-work appears in the vault-beam data and is discussed below.

Two surviving subspring beams are present in Rm. 1 at 1.80 m from the ends of the room (Fig. 65b). Both are unmodified logwood beams, ca. 0.15 m in diameter, with no obvious wear marks.

The final CS. 6 operation probably consisted of room floors. These are noticeable in one place only: on section/profile line B-B', where they are poorly preserved (probably eroded by the acid in bat dung). They are soft, of small pulverized limestone chunks covered with a thin white plaster that turns up onto primary wall plaster.

Stage 5: Vaults of the Building

Stage 5 includes the work following wall construction: wooden lintels over doorways, medial corbels, vault masonry, and plastering of the vault back and sub-roof.

Setting of the lintels over doorway openings constituted the first step in vault construction; there is no visible pause-line between supra-lintel and vault material. The lintels rest on previously plastered beds at varying distances below the wall tops. In Dr. 16, a full course of supra-lintel masonry was necessary to fill the gap over the lintels to wall-top level, but in Dr. 15 soffit headers rest directly on lintel beams.

The 10 surviving lintels consist of unworked log-wood beams (in one case still retaining bark) averaging 0.10 m in diameter, and varying in number of beams from 7 to 13. Butts are concealed behind masonry plastered flush with the wall face.

It is theorized that before the placement of vault masonry could begin, a timber false-work structure was built within each room. Vertical poles or masts, erected in the centers of the rooms, extended up through the gap where capstones would be installed after the timbers had been removed. The masts could have been anchored to horizontal beams built into the walls (as in Rm. 8; Fig. 29c) and to diagonal bracing poles. Horizontal vault beams would be fixed to the vertical masts and thus placed in position prior to masonry construction. This timber structure could have served for false-work and scaffolding during vault construction.

Vaults survive intact over all five rooms in the rear range. They have fallen partially at outer doorways in the front range. All surviving vaults are six courses high with approximately 8 cm outset springs at a uniform level corresponding with the wall-top plaster. A three-stepped soffit profile (Fig. 25; 26 and Pl. 65b) appears in the five rooms of the front range; all others are straight or slightly convex.

Dimensions and shapes of vault masonry are standardized and closely controlled (Table 18). Stones are facially square and identical in longitudinal and end vaults. Thicknesses are more variable. All stones are tapered in plan and section to a well-rounded butt and tightly packed in good quality mortar. Coursing is regular, but is not reflected as layering in vault cores. Mortar joints are thin at the soffit face and spalls are rare.

Face surfaces were dressed after placement of headers, before the setting of capstones. In the stepped vaults, the soffit profile was also cut after header placement. A thin white plaster was applied to the soffit faces, also before the capstones were installed, as shown by a plaster turnover from the top of the soffit to the capstone bed. At the bottom of the vaults, the plaster feathered out onto the previously finished wall plaster.

Capstones average approximately 0.22 m in height, 0.34 to 0.50 m in width, and 0.80 m in length, squared

Table 18
Structure 5C-13
Depths of Vault Beam Sockets (m)

	Number	Mean (m)	Standard Deviation	Range (m)
Upper	41	0.48	15.4	0.23–0.82
Middle	22	0.54	22.8	0.27–0.93
Lower	31	0.64	20.6	0.32–1.10

except for the ends, and preplastered over the central strip of the underside. The cap width between soffits is 0.20 m in the front range and 0.18 in the rear.

Vault-back facings (separating the vault core from the upper-zone core) consist of small, roughly shaped and coursed stones facially dressed after placement. Erosion has removed all traces of plaster from the vault back itself, but a hard plaster subroof (Fig. 25:4) is probably the extension of vault-back plaster over the capstones to seal the building during upper-zone construction. At the base of the vault back (Fig. 25:7), a similar hard plaster coating turns out onto the tops of the medial corbels, probably hardened by the weight of the upper-zone masonry. Medial corbel stones consistently taper to a narrow butt with hard mortar tightly parked into the spaces between.

Beam sockets figure in all surviving longitudinal vaults. A total of 19 unmodified logwood beams remain more or less intact (Fig. 27–29; 65b). Several now-empty socket holes indicate that the ends of the beams had been forked, perhaps for better anchorage. In the case of socket 8 in Rm. 8, the hole seems to have been formed by two beams lashed together, with one at an angle like a bracing member.

Diameters of 116 beams and sockets range from 0.07 to 0.14 m, mean value 0.10 m, standard deviation 1.80, indicating strong predominance of a value close to the mean. Depths, on the other hand, vary greatly as shown in Table 18. Lower level beams penetrate more deeply into vault core, but no beam passes entirely through the core mass. This implies that vault construction proceeded room by room through the building. The three vault beam levels do not correspond to the course levels of vault masonry, indicating that the beams were first placed on a timber frame and the vault masonry was built up around them.

Stage 4: Roof and Upper Zone of the Building

The roof is composed of 0.24 m of rubble aggregate in a good quality gray mortar topped by thin white plaster that runs under the upper story (Fig. 25:3). The upper zone survives for about two-thirds of its full height across most of the rear façade and at the corners of the lateral side extension in the front façade. The front profile obtained at the side (Fig. 25) is assumed for the axial profile in Fig. 24. There was no surviving sculpture in the front, but the extant portions are not in corners or over doorways where sculpture is expected. The rear façade contains four rectangular sculptured panels (Fig. 65a), all badly eroded, but apparently repeating the same motif: a

human face beneath a projecting headdress or mask. The N rear lateral side extension upper zone has diagonally projecting stones (Fig. 64d) that suggest a corner mask. If present, then very likely all corners had masks—a possibility not illustrated in Fig. 23c.

Upper-zone facings consist of veneer stones, which are thinner than wall-facing stones (0.15–0.18 m thick and 0.20–0.30 m high). No plaster survives except perhaps in the rear where upper-zone surfaces were too high to examine.

Stage 3: Walls and Building Platform of the Upper Story

The plastered roof survives only beneath upper-story material and the area examined was too small to ascertain the degree of weathering, in order to indicate whether or not the upper story was a primary component.

The unplastered surface of the upper-story building platform indicates that there was little or no pause before wall construction, thus the two features are included together in CS. 3 Presumably, CS. 3 was finished by wall and wall-top plaster as in the lower building.

The building platform is 0.60 m high and its upper surface projects 0.30 m from the wall. Facing stones had eroded in the small area examined (Fig. 25), and therefore the slight batter shown is speculative.

Upper-story walls survive only to about 0.40 m high but provide enough data for a conclusive plan (Fig. 23a). Exterior facings are thin veneer stones (ca. 0.14 m) shaped to a precise rectangular form on all principal surfaces (butts as well as faces). The faces had probably been dressed after placement. Interior facings are identical. No room floors were encountered and no plaster remains on accessible features.

Stage 2: Upper-Story Vaults

The thickness and disposition of the walls point to the existence of vaulting in the upper story. No vault stones were actually seen in the upper-story debris and in fact rubble depth is not particularly great. The bulk of vault material must have fallen off the roof, perhaps thrown outward by tree-growth and uprooting patterns.

Stage 1: Roof and Upper Zone of the Upper Story

Inferred upper-story vaulting implies a roof and upper zone, although no debris could be identified as upper-zone material. The form of the upper zones as shown in Fig. 23c repeats that of the building without corner masks.

Modifications

Interior platforms U. 2 and 3 (Fig. 23b; 26a; 29c) in Rm. 7 and 9 are interpreted as secondary additions (if only a matter of days) on the basis of wall plaster abutment (floors were not accessible). Both exhibit smoothly finished plaster surfaces and a high standard of workmanship compatible with that of the primary building.

Units 4 and 5 (Fig. 23b:2, 3) are vertical plaster turns that run between secondary holes in the jambs of Dr. 10 and 16. They indicate that permanent plastered screens closed these doorways, altering the circulation pattern of the building. Unit 6 in Dr. 6 (Fig. 23b:3) is probably an unplastered door-closing device determined by secondary beam sockets approximately 0.10 m deep.

In Rm. 9, VB 5 (Fig. 27) has a mortar sleeve in its E socket that could have resulted from beam replacement. The secondary beam evidently tapered from a thick end, equivalent to the original beam diameter, to a thinner end that required the sleeve. The careful replacement argues for its occurrence during the Classic Period, yet the tapering might allude to a shortage of uniform wooden members or reduced circumstances of the occupants. In Rm. 1 (Fig. 28) the W socket of VB. 10 had been sealed with a well-made plaster plug smoothly finished to match the vault soffit. This loss of a vault beam, not replaced, again may imply reduced circumstances.

Relation to Adjacent Stratigraphy

The coherent organization of the 5C-13 group argues that all three structures and the platform that sustains them represent a single construction. The group platform abuts the larger southern platform that sustains the earlier Str. 5D-77, 5C-54, and 5C-49. To the N, it adjoins the larger platform that sustains Temple III and may be associated with the Tozzer Causeway. Stela 24 in front of the temple carries a dedicatory date of 9.19.0.0.0 and the style date of Li. 2 of Temple III is 9.19.0.0.0 + 2.5 katuns (TR. 33A:52, 55). Temple III, crowded in front of the Str. 5C-13 group, looks like a late intrusive element on this platform. Thus, 5C-13 appears earlier than Temple III and perhaps is contemporary with the Tozzer Causeway and Temple IV, which has wooden lintels with dates of 9.15.10.0.0 (TR. 33A:101).

Table 19
Structure 5C-13: Time Spans

Time Span	Unit and Floor	Comment
1		Abandonment and collapse
2		Use inferred
3	U. 1–6	Interior platforms; doorway screens
4		Use inferred
5		CS. 1–6; ca. 11,300 m^3

Architecture

Accepting reconstructions shown in Fig. 23 with the caveats outlined above, Str. 5C-13 represents a highly coherent architectural form. It has five components: supplementary platform; building platform; building; upper-story building platform; and upper-story building. Because building platforms are so suppressed, three major visual units emerge that include the supplementary platform; the building and its building platform; and the upper story as a whole. All three have approximately the same total heights and follow the same plan configuration. The resulting composition has great visual strength and order.

Both the lower building and upper story have five doorways in the front façade separated by interjamb spaces that progressively decrease with distance from the axis. This spacing pattern has been created by placing the lower non-axial doorways eccentrically in the rooms they access. In fact, no doorway facing E in the lower building occupies the center of any room space except for the two axial doorways, whereas all upper-story doorways appear to be centralized. Only the axial doorways are aligned between the building and the upper story.

The upper story has another distinguishing feature: aligned front and rear doorways in two pairs flanking the principal axis. If the system were at building level, the arrangement would allow through-circulation as in an entry to a courtyard or plaza. In an upper story, however, through-circulation to the narrow rear ledge would hardly seem important. Perhaps these openings have astronomical significance relating to a viewing point in the courtyard to the E. This might, in fact, explain the extensive platform-sustaining structure and the large open space to the E of it.

The rooms and doorways in the lower building (as initially built) established three distinct room systems or suites: one central and two lateral ones. All rooms in each suite are linked by interior doorways, yet it is necessary to go outside to pass between suites. The axial rooms are 24% longer than those flanking them in the suite, 19% longer than adjacent rooms in the lateral suites, 16% longer than the transverse end rooms. Evidently, room length differentials as axial references were used where they would be most readily perceptible and therefore most effective.

Modifications subsequently changed the pattern of suites. In the axial suite, R. 7 came to be isolated by a permanent doorway seal that blocked through-circulation, possibly for the storage of valuable objects. If so, then the bench (U. 2) that almost fills the room might relate to the same function, providing a surface at a higher level than any of the room floors. The bench in Rm. 9 (U. 3) looks like a monumental throne (Fig. 29b: Bn. 2). Nonetheless its position in the room, with no aligned doorway and almost no space clear in front, seems ill-suited for an audience function.

The upper story entirely lacks interior circulation. The axial room is only 2% longer than the rooms that flank it and only 6% longer than the two outer rooms in the same range. Once again, as with doorway and room space relationships, axial emphasis appears greater in the lower building than in the upper story.

Front to rear asymmetry appears in the lack of rear stairs and doorways, the lesser rear lateral side extensions, offset placement of transverse doorways, placement of "windows" in the rear façade only, placement of upper story on the rear part of the building, stepped vault profile in front range only, and thinned walls at the front. Some symmetry exists in equal first- and second-range room widths, central doorway placement in the side rooms, and identical vault-beam patterns in all rooms except for two added beams in the rear axial room.

Attributes that imply a late construction date for Str. 5C-13 include absence of a floor running under the walls of the building; visual suppression of the building platform; plastered wall tops; preplastered capstones; plastered vault back; thin, white plaster, one coat only; veneer facing stones; tapered vault headers; dressing of masonry surfaces after setting of stones; wide walls relative to height; and high vaults and upper zones relative to wall height. There are no early features that conflict with these.

8

Group 5D-14: "South Acropolis"

Group 5D-14 comprises Str. 5D-100 through 104 and 141, together with Plat. 5D-30. Collectively these features have been known as the "South Acropolis." The group was first mapped by Maler in 1904, delineating the rooms of the four quadrangle buildings and central temple (1971: Fig. 39). Tozzer (1911: Fig. 35, 36; 122–124) added to this the group designation "southern Acropolis" and room plans of Str. 5D-100, 102, and 103. Eight structure numbers 44–51 were utilized by Tozzer for the complex.

The Tikal map (TR. 11) appointed one structure number for each of the four sides of the acropolis summit. Only one additional designation is presently required, 5D-141 on the E side of the quadrangle (Fig. 30).

All structures are shown in TR. 11 hatched as standing architecture, yet physical preservation is poor. Only the western structure, 5D-100, retains standing vault elements. Wall remnants and mound contours of the others provide complete plans, but little else. Although no plan is possible for Str. 5D-14, it was included in order to complete the picture for this distinctive group.

The group was interpreted by Tozzer (1911:124) as "an artificially levelled hill," an understandable reaction to its magnitude. Tozzer's plan (his sketch map) accordingly showed only summit features and omitted the sustaining platform. Maler's rediscovered Tikal map (1975) suggests the height and terracing of the platform. The TR. 11 map shows that the platform was approached by a northern stairway only, and indicates a complexity of terracings on the E face. The architectural survey picked up some details representing these components of Plat. 5D-30 (Fig. 31), but not enough to elucidate plan configuration.

The group on top of the Acropolis makes up a rectangular perimeter of single-story, range-type structures (Fig. 30), tightly enclosing a pyramidal "temple." On the basis of surface features, it is difficult to know which side of the quadrangle might be its front of principal entry. Platform 5D-30 appears to have wide, inset stairs on its N side and the summit pyramid (Str. 5D-104) also faces N; however, the northernmost building of the quadrangle, Str. 5D-101, does not show entry features. Rather it is the western structure, 5D-100, that suggests formal entry, and the Acropolis platform extends out in a broader W terrace, which argues for frontality toward the large westward plaza. Thus, Gp. 5D-14 may have a double front, one aspect facing W toward Str. 5C-54, and another facing N toward the Great Plaza and the North Acropolis.

During the 1968 survey, Orrego recorded a surface profile (fig. 31a) based on collapse debris and exposed terrace facings off-center on the N side. This profile shows a probable four terraces. The lower three have apron and basal moldings. Facing masonry is illustrated in elevation for the second terrace (Fig. 31b). Masonry attributes are not significantly different from substructure facings on top of the Acropolis.

Structure 5D-100

The W wing of the summit quadrangle is enclosed almost entirely by Str. 5D-100 (Fig. 32a; 33–35c; 65d–67b), a one-story, range-type building with unusually large lateral transverse extensions. Previous plans of the building are by Maler in 1904 (1974: Fig. 39) and Tozzer and Merwin in 1910 (Tozzer 1911: Fig. 35). Its vaults have fallen except for fragments at the ends of some rooms and where the whole N end set of rooms had been filled.

Table 20
Structure 5D-100
Facing-Stone Dimensions (m)

	Number	Mean (m)	Standard Deviation	Range (m)
Exterior wall width	40	0.54	0.40–0.82	9.22
Exterior wall height	40	0.16	0.12–0.24	2.42
Half-vault width	40	0.08	0.18–0.42	3.91
Half-vault height	40	0.17	0.13–0.26	2.66
Half-vault depth	18	0.57	0.48–0.74	6.79
End-vault depth	–	0.57	0.33–0.75	9.38

Recording was by Loten in 1966 without excavation. Later, in 1968, Orrego partially cleared the SE corner of the substructure and his data are included here (Fig. 34c, d). The N rooms of the building were inaccessible and were reconstructed to be identical with the S rooms. Because debris forced measurement at differing heights and the walls are not vertical, recorded plan-lines frequently did not meet and Fig. 32a rectifies this in broken-line.

The structure is described in Tozzer (1911:123, his structure 51) and mapped by Maler (174: Fig. 39) as having four ranges of rooms and no lateral side extensions, whereas our Fig. 32a shows two ranges and large extensions. The discrepancy may result from the presence of secondary exterior walls, now obscured by collapse, but discernable as low ridges perpendicular to the main walls. These hint at substantial secondary construction, but would require excavation beyond the scope of this survey to determine their true significance. Therefore, 5D-100 is reported here as unmodified except for the filling of rooms in the N end of the building.

Construction Stages

Stage 3: Supplementary Platform

Initial work on Str. 5D-100 began with a supplementary platform approximately 2.50 m high (Fig. 34c, d; 66a). Excavations stopped at an abutting platform floor near its base. A hard, smooth, plaster top surface runs under the building platform. The supplementary platform is rectangular, rather than conforming to the building plan. The stairs on the E and W sides imply axial ingress into the group. The S stairs are suggested by debris profiles, whereas those at the N are assumed. The SE corner is sharp, rather than rounded, and all other corners are drawn accordingly.

Facing masonry of the supplementary platform is distinctly superior to that of the building (Fig. 34d). Stones are well shaped to a rectangular face and are consistently coursed. Heights vary from 0.17 to 0.28 m, whereas stretchers average 0.28 m in width. Stone depths generally exceed heights and therefore the facing could be classified as "block" masonry rather than "slab." The small area of exposed surface contains no traces of surviving plaster.

Stage 2: Building Platform

The building platform is a low masonry component sustained on the plaster top of the supplementary platform (Fig. 65d; 66a). Its upper surface could not be identified at the exterior, but is assumed to equate with Floor 1 in Rm. 9 that runs under the interior faces of the building walls and evidently served as both the primary and only room floor (Fig. 34a). It has a fine-grained, hard, smooth topping 2- to 3-cm thick on 0.10 m of small stone ballast. Building-platform facing consists of two courses of stones similar to those of the interior walls. Face batter appears to have been cut after the stones had been set in place.

Stage 1: Building

Despite the size of the building (ca. 519 m^2), the whole ensemble of walls, vaults, and upper zones appears to have been built without major pauses (Fig. 34b; 35b). Walls stand on the building-platform floor, above which there are no other plastered surfaces (wall tops, preplastered capstones, or vault backs). Wall tops are marked, however, by a soft layer of unplastered mortar signifying a leveling operation preparatory to vaulting.

The 18 primary rooms are apparently all at the same floor level with two axial ranges and two ranges in each lateral side extension. The N lateral rooms eventually were packed with coursed block and rubble masonry to the capstones.

The little exterior wall masonry that could be seen is of better quality and finish than that of the interior. Outer surfaces were dressed after construction. Interior facings, clearly not dressed after construction, are subrectangular (round-edged), horizontally laid slabs. Course levels only run for short distances. Butt surfaces are not consistently tapered or squared. Widths average 0.54 m, heights, 0.16 m (Table 20). Depths are generally greater than heights, heights more consistent than widths. Headers are indistinguishable from stretchers in shape. Their heights are also more closely controlled than widths, and depths generally exceed heights. Joints are thick, from 2 to 10 cm. Spalls are frequent, 5 to 10 cm in length, and almost filling the joints at 12 to the meter.

All interior plaster has vanished from chambers with standing vault fragments, but remains in good condition in the S end rooms with completely collapsed vaults. In Rm. 8, plaster is smooth and white: a thin coat on a thick mortar base that smoothed out irregularities in the masonry. The surface retains a faint pinkish hue that may indicate red paint.

The small Dr. 5, 11, 12, and 22 are vaulted (with outset springs; Fig. 32a; 34a). Collapsed Dr. 1-4, 8, 10, 13, 15, and 21 present debris profiles typical of wooden lintels. The opening designated as Dr. 14 (Fig. 32a; 67a) has a horizontal stone slab lintel similar to those over exterior windows. It may, in fact, be a window because debris obscures it to lintel level. Window-like openings are visible in Rm. 10 and 15 (Fig. 32a) and are also inferred in Rm. 4, 5, and 14 from collapse patterns (not in plan).

In the W end wall of Rm. 8 are three small rectangular niches 0.10 m deep, 0.20 m wide, and 0.17 m high (Fig. 66c). Another occurs in the E end of the same room (Fig. 66d) and two others in the vault. These recesses do not seem to have housed subspring beams. All, except those subject to weathering above the debris level, are neatly finished with primary wall plaster.

In Rm. 9, two pairs of holes ca. 0.15 m square in section penetrate the exterior wall at wall top and bottom (Fig. 34a). They appear in Fig. 32a to the point where they are filled with debris. Unplastered, they are best interpreted as scaffolding holes. No other wall surfaces were accessible at mid-height, so it is likely that other holes remain undetected.

The best-preserved accessible vaulting is at the S end of Rm. 9 (Fig. 34a). Vaulting remains intact in the N lateral extension, but is not visible. In Rm. 9, and in oth-

Table 21
Structure 5D-100: Time Spans

Time Span	Unit and Floor	Comment
1		Abandonment and collapse
2		Continued use inferred
3		Filling in of N end rooms; secondary rooms in front of E and W facades
4		Use inferred
5	Fl. 1, 2	CS. 1-3; ca. 4,000 m^3

er scattered vault fragments in the building (Fig. 35a), profiles are irregular, shifting from concave to convex. Spring outsets, all at a constant level, vary from 0.10 m to an almost imperceptible line. End soffits are far less inclined than longitudinal ones. The vault is eight courses high in Rm. 3 and nine courses in Rm. 9, although the two vault heights are similar. Mortar joints are 4 to 8 cm thick.

Vault headers are flat and relatively unspecialized in shape. Heights (Table 20) show more variability than widths. End-vault facing stones are mostly stretchers, as seen in Fig. 34a. Their larger dimension (average 0.57 m) is similar to that of wall facings and soffit headers. Headers and stretchers were probably not differentiated in the quarrying, but only in the setting and the cutting of the face angle. End vaults appear to be all stretchers, and long vaults include a scattered few.

Soffit angles appear to have been cut prior to setting. In most cases, the angle is less steep than that of the soffit itself, as if the angle had been cut with the stone horizontal and then placed at a slight angle with the butt raised. This suggests specialized labor, one crew of stone cutters to prepare the stones and another of masons to set them in place. Tool marks from hard stone mauls are visible in many stone faces. In the E vault of Rm. 3, one stone, obviously reused from an earlier structure, retains a layer of hard smooth plaster on its surface.

Capstones are relatively large (ca. 1 m in length) and most are preplastered. Cap width varies from 0.14 to 0.30 m in Rm. 3 and 9. A vertical task line in the vault mass between these two rooms (Fig. 35a) indicates that the Rm. 9 vault was finished first.

Vault-beam holes were observed only in Rm. 9 (Fig. 34b). Neither beams nor stumps remain. Diameters vary from 0.08 to 0.13 m; depths from 0.30 to 1.05 m.

Although beam shapes appear to be roughly circular, they are not well delineated because of mortar and plaster loss.

Upper zones have fallen everywhere, although some fragments may remain beneath debris at the N end. A short stretch of medial molding on the W side is two courses high. Its profile is depicted in Fig. 35a, c.

Modifications

Debris mounds along the E and W facades suggest the existence of secondary transverse walls on the supplementary platform roughly following the room divisions of the building. These features were too unclear to be recorded in 1966, but were apparently more visible during Maler's and Tozzer's visits and appear on both plans (Maler 1974: Fig. 39; Tozzer 1911: Fig. 35). The debris ridges reveal no specialized wall or vault stones and are not large enough in volume to include collapsed vaults.

The only other modification noted is the filling in of Rm. 11–15 in the N lateral extension. The material employed for this purpose is visible through Dr. 14 and through an animal burrow on the roof of Rm. 13. Apparently, it consists entirely of well-cut cushion-shaped blocks horizontally bedded in good quality mortar. The standard of workmanship implies a Classic Period operation.

Relation to Adjacent Stratigraphy

A layer of material at least 0.40-m thick surfaced by hard, smooth plaster (identified as Pl. 5D-30: Fl. 2 in Fig. 34c) abuts the supplementary platform at the SE corner and clearly postdates it. Unit 1, about 0.40 m thick, overlies it, its probable floor surface entirely disintegrated. This still-later floor might relate to a surface feature such as 5D-104.

Structure 5D-100, then, is earlier than at least one and probably two plate 5D-30 floors, either of which might have been built with other Acropolis structures such as 5D-104. Indeed, the configuration of structures on the Acropolis does not suggest the kind of unified organization that might be expected had all the structures been built at the same time.

Architecture

Structure 5D-100 is H-shaped, a multi-chambered range-type building with doorways on both facades, standing on a relatively low substructure, and apparently lacking upper-story or roof-structure components. Although the facades differ in several details, neither appears to be the front and we have arbitrarily assigned the front to the E façade.

The alignment of Dr. 1, 2, and 3 creates an open passage through the building axis and suggests that this part of the edifice provided a formal ingress to the quadrangle as a whole. A similar alignment links Dr. 13, 15, and 21 just north of axis, but not Dr. 4, 5, and 11 to the S. The size and complexity of the building suggests that the axial entry constituted only part of the whole functional program served by 5D-100.

While the E exterior presents symmetry in its central part flanked by two deeply projecting lateral side extensions, the interior circulation pattern seems less formally structured. The central rooms connect internally with the N one. The positioning of interior doorways in the central ranges is irregular.

Room 7, and its assumed counterpart, R. 17, are distinctively the only ones not linked to several others. Doorways 4 and 21 are placed farther away from the axis than they would have been if they had occupied the centers of the chambers they serve. This visually isolates the axial opening in a larger stretch of wall and gives it greater visual impact. At the same time, the axial doorway is left as the only one "centered" in any sense. Another possible emphasis on the axis is the fact that axial Rm. 1 and 2 exceed the lengths of other rooms by 28.8%. The apparent violation of Dr. 11 seems odd. Could this be an expression of frontality for the eastern façade?

Early attributes of the structure include presence of a floor running under the building walls; absence of a vault-back surface; dressing of wall and vault facing stones prior to their setting rather than afterward; vaults and upper zones relatively low in relation to wall heights; and relatively long, narrow proportions of axial rooms. Late attributes include the low single-terrace building platform; masonry surfaces dressed after setting on the building platform and supplementary platform; and thick building walls. In general, the substructure appears more progressive in form and technique than the building.

Structure 5D-101

The N side of the Gp. 5D-14 quadrangle is encompassed by Str. 5D-101 (Figs. 30; 32b; 35b). Its vaults are almost entirely fallen, its rooms filled with debris, and its substructural components completely buried. The structure is mentioned briefly by Maler in his Peabody

Table 22
Structure 5D-101
Facing-Stone Dimensions (m)

	Number	Mean (m)	Standard Deviation	Range (m)
Exterior wall width	100	0.54	14.58	0.30–0.96
Exterior wall height	100	0.19	4.68	0.10–0.39
Interior wall width	38	0.47	12.29	0.25–0.69
Interior wall height	38	0.155	2.60	0.11–0.20
Vault width	9	0.26	4.08	0.16–0.32
Vault height	9	0.16	3.83	0.11–0.25

Museum report (1911:51) and mapped in detail in his Tikal plan (1971: Plan 39); Tozzer shows it as two structures (1911: Pl. 29; Str. 49 and 50). Orrego recorded it in the Tikal Project architectural survey in 1968 and excavated a small trench between 5D-101 and 5D-141 to reveal substructural details.

Construction Stages

Only one construction stage is noticeable, apparently including the building platform, building walls, and vaults. Upper-zone and roof elements have all fallen and surviving fragments do not reveal whether these were built as a separate stage. The amount of debris in and around the building is not enough to suggest an upper story.

The building platform rests on a plastered surface (Pl. 5D-30: Fl. 1; Fig. 35b) of the Acropolis with no evidence of a supplementary platform. The platform itself has a moderate batter with neither apron nor basal moldings. Facing masonry is similar to that of the building walls. Stairs are not evident in debris profiles.

The building walls stand on an unplastered mortar bed atop the building platform. Exterior facing masonry consists of subrectangular (round-edged) slabs laid horizontally, not consistently coursed, and not specialized as headers or stretchers. It resembles closely that of Str. 5D-100. Exterior facing stones average 0.54 in width by 0.19 m in height with little dimensional standardization (Table 22). Mortar joints are thick and spalls frequent. Exposed surfaces appear to have been individually dressed prior to installation. No traces of wall plaster survive. Interior and exterior facings are essentially identical.

Vault masonry, as indicated by a single surviving fragment (Fig. 35b), closely resembles wall material in size, shape, and positioning, only narrower (0.26 by 0.16 m average) and perhaps more consistently coursed (Table 22). The vault spring is at the same level as the medial corbel. Together these are the only features that define the unplastered wall top. The amount of vault masonry still in place is too small to provide information about soffit profiles, vault beams, capstones, or vault backs. Fallen vault stones are not recognizable in the debris.

The upper zones have a medial molding (Fig. 35b); there is no surviving upper-zone plaster or indication of sculptural treatment.

The building originally consisted of Rm. 1-8 (Fig. 32b), presumably all at the same level. Debris within the rooms conceals any evidence of benches or other features.

Modifications

Rooms 9-13, on the NE corner of the building, constitute major modifications. These presumably stand on an undetermined secondary extension of the building platform. Wall masonry of the five-room addition abuts primary walls at two points: on the SE corner and on the N façade. Architectural attributes (including masonry) do not differ from those of the primary structure.

Inside the building, the only visible modification is

Table 23
Structure 5D-101: Time Spans

Time Span	Unit and Floor	Comment
1		Abandonment and collapse
2		Use inferred
3	U. 1	Rm. 9-13; narrowing of Dr. 9; ca. 700 m³
4		Use inferred
5		Construction; ca. 2,000 m³

U. 1 (Fig. 32b), a secondary doorjamb in Dr. 9 between Rm. 1 and 6. The extent of collapse makes it impossible to determine whether U. 1 was associated with lintel-beam replacement over the doorway or installed simply to reduce the size of the extraordinarily wide doorway. Masonry attributes are not significantly different from primary wall facings.

Relation to Adjacent Stratigraphy

Under Str. 5D-101 is Pl. 5D-30: Fl. 1, perhaps equivalent to U. 1 or Fl. 2 abutting Str. 5D-100. Structure 5D-142 appears to be an addition.

Architecture

Structure 5D-101 in its primary form is a one-story, range-type entity with four end rooms and doorways on both long facades, lacking side extensions and upper story.

The building defies identification of the front or the principal axis. Doorway 1 is close to the original center of the building, but Dr. 8 in the S façade is more than a meter E of its line. Transverse end Rm. 3, 4, 7, and 8 balance each other symmetrically about Dr. 1, but the longitudinal rooms seem to ignore this center entirely.

Both facades have some frontal attributes. The N façade has the best-balanced composition of doorways with intervening wall segments varied to emphasize the wider central opening. The S façade has near its center an even wider opening, Dr. 8, aligned with interior Dr. 9. The eccentric positioning of Dr. 10 and 7 around Dr. 8, on the other hand, is more typical of a rear façade.

Some characteristics of 5D-101 suggest an early date of construction. These include absence of wall-top plaster; unspecialized vault masonry; face dressing of masonry before installation and wide rooms relative to wall thickness. Other attributes are characteristic of late buildings: horizontally laid, subrectangular wall-facing stones; and the use of stretchers in vault soffits.

As modified by the addition of Rm. 9-13, the building is even more asymmetric than the primary structure. These rooms form two extensions from the original building, each with doorways providing aligned circulation through Dr. 19, 20, and 21, and partly aligned through Dr. 16, 17, and 18 (resembling the arrangement of Dr. 1, 8, and 9). Presence of a formal entry to the quadrangle from its W side through Str. 5D-100, and the location of the main Acropolis stairway on its N side, might have created a need for circumferential circulation through or around the secondary features of 5D-101 (Fig. 30).

Table 24
Structure 5D-102: Time Spans

Time Span	Unit and Floor	Comment
1		Abandonment and collapse
2		Use inferred
3		Rm. 5; ca. 160 m^3
4		Use inferred
5		Construction; ca. 550 m^3

Structure 5D-102

The E side of the summit quadrangle is formed by Str. 5D-102 (Fig. 36), together with 5D-141 and a northern extension off the E end of 5D-103 (Fig. 30). It appears in the Tikal Project map as contiguous with 5D-103 (TR. 11), but in fact there is a narrow alleyway between the two. Maler's 1904 Tikal plan (1971: Plan 39) delineates the rooms without much accuracy and as though joined with 5D-103. Tozzer also joins 5D-102 with 5D-103 (1911: Fig. 36) and shows a secondary eastward extension from 5D-102 as a separate structure (ibid., Pl. 29; "Structures 44 and 45"). He describes his secondary addition as being "on a terrace slightly lower than the general level" (ibid., p. 124), something no longer recognizable. When the Tikal Project map was made, the lack of preservation of the eastward addition prevented its inclusion.

Structure 5D-102 was recorded by Orrego in 1968. His plan (Fig. 36) is based in part on interpretation of debris contours. Vaults have fallen completely and wall masonry projects only slightly above debris in a few places. No data are available beyond the plan of the building at debris-surface level, although it is evident that Rm. 5 is a secondary construction.

Architecture

Range-type and without lateral side extensions, Str. 5D-102 has a symmetrical room arrangement of two axial chambers flanked by transverse ones, all entered through a single exterior doorway. Because of this doorway, the front can be identified as the W façade facing into the quadrangle.

The addition of Rm. 5 ignores the axial symmetry of the primary structure. The aligned doorways in this addition permit through-passage and circulation around the circumference of the Acropolis. This addition may be a formal continuation of a movement pattern that existed from the outset.

Table 25
Structure 5D-103
Facing-Stone Dimensions (m)

	Number	Mean (m)	Standard Deviation	Range (m)
Exterior wall width	100	0.54	14.37	0.27-0.98
Exterior wall height	100	0.17	2.97	0.10-0.25
Interior wall width	7	0.51	7.22	0.36-0.62
Interior wall height	7	0.16	1.81	0.13-0.19
Vault width	7	0.26	2.06	0.22-0.29
Vault height	7	0.15	2.23	0.13-0.19

Structure 5D-103

Extending across the S side of the South Acropolis quadrangle (Fig. 30), Str. 5D-103 (Fig. 37a) wraps itself around the SE corner. Maler (1971: Plan 39) drew an incorrect plan of the rooms. Tozzer (1911: Fig. 36) also presented some detail and a relatively correct room plan. Vaults are completely fallen and rooms are filled with debris, although not to a depth sufficient to suggest the presence of an upper story. The present record was gathered in 1968 by Orrego without excavation. From the plan configuration (Fig. 37a), it appears likely that the E wing is a secondary addition to a symmetrical building. Careful inspection failed, however, to reveal a primary /secondary joint and the structure is therefore reported as unmodified.

Table 26
Structure 5C-103: Time Spans

Time Span	Unit and Floor	Comment
1		Abandonment and collapse
2		Use inferred
3		Construction; ca. 1,700 m³

Construction Stages

Only a single construction stage is distinguishable by surface features, which are the walls and the vaults of the building. Presumably a roof and upper zone were present, but whether they were built on a plastered vault back is not known. Substructure data are similarly unavailable.

Wall masonry consists of slab facings horizontally bedded, partially but not consistently, coursed and not specialized as headers or stretchers (Table 25). Specialized vault stones are not recognizable in the debris. Windows in the S façade are spanned by stone lintels as in Str. 5D-100.

Architecture

Structure 5D-103 is a range-type, single story, L-shaped building without lateral side extensions and with exterior doorways in only one principal façade. Since the E wing of the building is much longer than the S, the front of the building should probably be seen as the N façade. Neither of the two N doorways occupies the façade center, thus violating one of the strongest rules of Maya architecture, that the principal axis should be marked by a doorway. Although the arrangement of rooms in the S wing is strongly symmetrical, the front-rear axis occurs between Rm. 1 and 2. Similar absence of a central opening is seen in the window arrangement of the S façade.

An early characteristic of the structure is the absence of wall-top plaster. Masonry attributes, on the other hand, appear to be neither early, nor late.

Structure 5D-104

Structure 5D-104 (Fig. 37b–38) occupies most of the space contained within the quadrangle atop the South Acropolis. It is poorly preserved, as the upper building has fallen to below wall-top level, and the terraces are concealed beneath debris with portions of facings visible. The plan of the structure, even the building, cannot be determined, but because of its prominent position on one of the major architectural features at Tikal, such data as are available on the surface are described below.

Previous descriptions appear singularly at variance with the finding of the architectural survey. Maler refers to 5D-104 as a "small three-chambered temple (on) a pyramidal substructure" (1911:51). He describes the building component as only "partially in ruins" and indicates that "it had the typical threefold division" and

Table 27
Structure 5D-104
Wall Masonry Dimensions (m)

	Number	Mean (m)	Standard Deviation	Range (m)
Wall width	67	0.47	10.11	0.24–0.69
Wall height	67	0.15	2.38	0.09–0.21
Terrace width	12	0.37	4.54	0.28–0.44

"a stairway on its E side." His Tikal map (1971: Plan 39) reconstructs three rooms and an eastern stairway. Tozzer also saw the structure as facing E and represents it in his map (1911: Pl. 29; Str. 48) with side-insets in the walls of the building. These details all conflict with TR. 11, which places the stair on the N side and shows a small building with no side insets.

The 1968 survey by Loten confirms the finding of TR. 11. In this investigation, two small trenches were excavated to clarify features, one at plaza level near the NW corner of the substructure (Fig. 38a), and one on axis at the rear of the building (Fig. 38b). All features listed below as primary underlie secondary features. The reconstruction illustrated in Fig. 37b and the time-span table shows a likely relationship between features at the top and bottom of the substructure.

Construction Stages

Behind the lowermost terrace facing at one location, off center in the rear, stands a vertical terrace facing (Unit 1; Fig. 38b). Its masonry attributes are similar to those of the surface terraces. There is no evidence of demolition; U. 1 extends up to the debris surface and its poor condition could have occurred through collapse and erosion. Unit 1 is probably either an earlier structure or a construction wall built to consolidate the fill in preparation for the terrace 5D-104.

A horizontal plaster surface (Unit 4; Fig. 38b) extends at least 3 m along the face of the bottom substructural terrace in the rear. This indicates that the lower part of the terrace, including the lower apron with its surviving plaster, is an earlier feature to which the upper part has been added. The course of inset vertical stones rests on the plaster surface of U.4, which could connect with U.1 as early stages of the terrace.

A hard, weathered plaster surface (Unit 3; Fig. 37b, 38c) that turns up to the rear wall of the building should be the top surface of a building platform. Building platforms generally do not extend so far out from the wall, however, and this identification is not certain. Unit 5 is a horizontal plaster surface at the top

of a terrace facing, visible on the E side of the substructure. It is far to the E of U. 3 and is not known to run under that floor (as Fig. 37b might suggest). Its position is such that excavation would almost surely reveal it to have been covered by terracing masonry. This would make it equivalent to U. 1, a likely but not demonstrable conclusion. Associated facing masonry has moderate batter similar to surface terracing, but distinctly smaller facing stones. Units 5 and 1 might represent an early structure of roughly the same height as the 5D-104 terracing. Alternatively U. 5 could connect with the building and U. 3.

Terrace heights as estimated from visible portions and debris contours provide three terraces up to U. 5. They also suggest an outset stair on the N, but do not reveal the presence or absence of side outsets or stair-side outsets. A difference in apron levels (Fig. 38a, b) implies presence of a rear axial outset. The NW corner is sharp rather than rounded. A poorly preserved floor runs under the substructure terraces at the NW corner (Fig. 38a).

Facing masonry consists of subrectangular slab stones (Table 28), horizontally bedded but not consistently coursed and not specialized as headers and stretchers. Face surfaces seem to have been dressed before, not after, installation. Mortar joints are thick, and spalls absent. A single coat of thick plaster remains as scattered fragments under the apron corbels.

The building, like U. 3, is at least partially overlaid by U. 2 in the same way that U. 1 and 4 are overlain by the surface terraces of the final substructure.

Only a portion of the building wall is noticeable. The interior, completely filled with debris, apparently consists of a single room. The amount of debris present justifies the assumption of vaults, yet specialized vault stones were not recognized in collapsed material.

Exterior wall-facing masonry consists of flat stones, subrectangular on the face, horizontally bedded, but not consistently coursed and not specialized as headers and stretchers (i.e., like that of the other buildings). Depths greatly exceed heights. The high standard deviation of width (Table 27) indicates that dimensional standardization was not an important factor in the quarrying and cutting of these facing stones. The outer face of individual stones appears to have been dressed to a smooth finish before the stones were set in the wall and not afterward.

The rear wall of the building stands slightly more than 2 m high. This is probably close to the original full height, as illustrated in Fig. 37b. The steep debris slope from rear to front reflects complete collapse of the front wall and suggests the presence of more than one doorway in the front façade.

Secondary Features

Unit 2 (Fig. 37b, 38c) is a body of masonry abutting the rear building wall and overlying U. 3. Off-axis (Fig. 38c), it retains a near-vertical facing of rectangular, flat stones, horizontally bedded. At its foot a step-out makes a deeply projecting basal molding. Masonry attributes are not significantly different from primary features.

The architectural significance of U. 2 is unclear. It may have extended laterally the full length of the rear wall or resembled a rear axial outset, or was a buttress construction to shore up a collapsing rear wall.

Architecture

Structure 5D-104, as reconstructed in Fig. 37b, is a one-room "temple" on a moderately high substructure with a single stairway. The lower substructure platform defined by three terraces could be considered as either a supplementary platform or a small pyramid. The lower-substructural component does not have the formal attributes of a building platform, but fulfills an equivalent architectural role, visually sustaining the building.

The fact that the two sidewalls of the building have fallen almost completely suggests that they did not have the side-inset configuration reported by Maler and Tozzer. The number of corners involved in the side-inset form increases the stability of a wall to such an extent that it usually stands longer than others.

Architectural attributes appear typical of neither early nor late Tikal. Absence of a floor running under the walls of the building is the most distinctively late attribute among the few visible ones. Masonry characteristics do not substantiate lateness, but equally do not represent early work. The particular constellation of architectural attributes present in 5D-104 and the other South Acropolis structures may eventually emerge as a middle classic architectural complex, perhaps contemporary to the Ik Ceramic complex.

Table 28
Structure 5D-104: Time Spans

Time Span	Unit Floor	Comment
1		Abandonment and collapse
2		Use inferred
3	U. 2	Exterior rear future
4		Use inferred
5	U. 3	Terraces and building, perhaps just after U. 1, 4, 5
6		Use inferred
7		Pyramid or earlier structure

Relation to Adjacent Stratigraphy

The terraces of 5D-104 rest on a floor and are abutted by no other known features. Accordingly, the structure may represent one of the terminal developments on the Acropolis

Structure 5D-141

A small structure, 5D-141 (Fig. 32b), sits on the E side of the quadrangle (Fig. 30). Although Maler (1971: Plan 39) and Tozzer apparently saw it as an individual feature (1911: Pl. 29: Str. 40), it was mapped by the Tikal Project as a south-projecting wing of 5D-101. Orrego recorded it in the 1968 architectural survey and accorded it a separate designation: 5D-141 (Fig. 32b). Actually, its substructure abuts 5D-101, but its building component is freestanding.

Vault masonry has completely fallen; walls have partially fallen and protrude above debris in a few places. The plan depicted in Fig. 32b is probably correct, but the structure provides little additional data; construction stages are not determinable and there is no visible evidence of modification.

The substructure appears to be a vertical-faced platform approximately 1 m high (Fig. 32b). Its facing stones are large, rectangular-faced blocks horizontally bedded and probably consistently coursed (only a very short section was seen). Wall masonry data are not available without excavation.

Architecture

Structure 5D-141 is a single story, range-type building on a single-component substructure, without lateral side extensions, and with doorway openings in both principal facades.

The substructure, because it directly sustains the walls of the building, is equivalent to a building platform. Instead of conforming to the building plan, it extends farther N to abut the substructure of 5D-191. The building, as a result, is placed eccentrically on this platform and as an entity looks unbalanced. In this respect, it is perhaps questionable that it should be designated as a separate structure rather than an appendage of 5D-101.

Table 29
Structure 5D-141: Time Spans

Time Span	Unit Floor	Comment
1		Abandonment and collapse
2		Use inferred
3		Construction; ca. 350 m^3

The arrangement of doorways appears intended to provide through-circulation into the quadrangle, but indirectly by the offset of Dr. 2.

9

Structure 5D-105

Immediately to the E of Temple V, Str. 5D-105 (Figs. 39–41), 5D-106, and 5D-107 define three sides of a U-shaped quadrangle raised on a low platform. Structure 5D-105, which faces E, appears to be the principal building in this group, as it is the largest and the only one retaining any visible standing features. Maler describes the structure briefly (1911:50–51), calling it "El Palacio de Dos Aposentos con Bóvedas de Escalones," and drew a ground plan on his more recently published Tikal map (1971: Plan 39). As number 43 in Tozzer's map (1911: Pl. 29), the building appears isolated. He refers to it as "of the residential type" but provides no description (ibid., 122). Unfortunately, it is not well preserved, as the greater part of the vaults have fallen, filling the rooms with debris past wall-top level. Only some vault ends and the rear exterior wall face stand clear and the substructure is entirely concealed.

There did not appear to be any location at which limited excavations might significantly add to the visible features, hence the building was recorded without excavation of any kind. Surface features do not indicate the presence of earlier construction at the locus, nor any architectural modifications.

Construction Stages

Stage 3: Lower Substructure, Building Platform, and Walls

Inclusion of the entire substructure and building walls in the same stage of construction is indicated by the rough unplastered mortar layers (Fig. 41a: 5) between them. Completion of this phase is denoted by hard wall-top plaster. The mortar layers appear to represent leveling devices intended to establish bedding planes for the building platform and walls. They are not hard enough to have served as finishing and plastering of the units that they cap.

Substructural core masonry exposed by erosion consists of tightly packed, horizontally bedded rubble set in mortar. No facings are visible. A bulge in debris on the E (front) side hints at a stair occupying the central third of the building's length.

The building platform (Fig. 41a) is two courses high. It consists entirely of stretchers roughly 0.60 m long. As proof that surfaces had been dressed after both building platform and wall-facing masonry had been installed, a slight lip on some wall stones coincides with the top surface of the building platform and must have been left after removal of material in the face-dressing operation. The building platform face has a smooth finish in straight-line profile with only slight batter.

Exterior wall facings are consistently coursed with stretchers predominating over headers, although the latter are readily identifiable. Dimensions are highly standardized (low values for standard deviation in Table 30), mortar joints thin and spalls infrequent. Typical stretchers are of a thick veneer form, slightly turtle-backed. Exposed faces have been dressed after installation to a smooth, straight-line profile with batter of 0.10 in 2.60 m.

Interior wall facings, although largely hidden by debris, appear identical. Course levels extend from exterior to interior faces. Core masonry consists of small- to medium-sized unbedded rubble aggregate.

Table 30
Structure 5D-105
Facing-Stone Dimensions (m)

	Number	Mean (m)	Standard Deviation	Range (m)
Exterior wall width	100	0.59	3.92	0.51–0.71
Exterior wall height	100	0.32	1.94	0.26–0.38
Interior wall width	11	0.24	7.61	0.21–0.31
Interior wall height	11	0.29	3.09	0.20–0.35
Vault width	5	0.26	4.94	0.18–0.32
Vault height	5	0.29	6.74	0.24–0.42

Stage 2: Vaults

Only small fragments of vaulting remain standing over the rear and transverse walls. The front longitudinal vault units have fallen completely.

Wall-top plaster and vault-back facing (Fig. 41a) indicate that the vaults were built as a separate stage in construction. The initial vault masonry is a continuous supra-lintel course that bears directly on the wall-top plaster. Of the few stones visible, several on the rear wall contain small-drilled holes (Fig. 41a: 3) about 3 cm in diameter, resembling rod row holes. Unfortunately, not enough were visible to firmly identify a true rod row. Presumably, the supra-lintel masonry was installed on top of wooden lintels over the doorways, but all of these have collapsed.

The supra-lintel course includes medial corbels at the exterior face. They are large stones, (ca. 0.70 m deep, 0.30 m high, and 0.40 m wide), sharply tapered in plan to butt ends (ca. 0.14 m wide). On their top surface is a layer of dark mortar that marks the foot of the vault back.

Vault soffits four courses high are consistently coursed and were finished to a stepped profile after installation of the stones. Springs are outset about 0.10 m and soffit steps average approximately 8 cm. Longitudinal vault facings are exclusively headers, rectangular on the face with the greater dimension in the vertical (Table 30). They taper to a butt width of roughly 0.14 m on both top and bottom surfaces. End vaults are similar except for the presence of a few stretchers. Mortar joints are uniformly thin at the face and widen toward the butt ends of the stones.

The vault-back facing consists of small, horizontally bedded, flat slab stones only very roughly shaped and not dressed on the surface. There is no visible vault-back plaster.

Surviving vault fragments include no beam sockets, but are too small to establish absence of vault beams. Neither soffit plaster nor capstones have survived collapse and erosion.

Stage 1: Upper Zone and Roof

Some upper-zone material remains on the rear (W) façade of the building (Fig. 41a), with carved surface profiles that suggest a decorative inset panel near the central axis. The motif, however, could not be identified. There are no remaining traces of plaster or paint. The panel does not survive to full height. There is no information about the upper molding or the roof, and the amount of debris does not seem to suggest a roof structure or upper story.

Relation to Adjacent Stratigraphy

Behind 5D-105, debris abuts the slope of the terrace supporting Temple V and appears to represent collapse subsequent to the erosion of the terrace face. Although 5D-105 abuts 5D-107, there is no clear indication that one is earlier than the other. Structures 5D-113, 114, and 106 also seem to be associated with 105 in the U-shaped east-facing group.

Table 31
Structure 5D-105: Time Spans

Time Span	Unit and Floor	Comment
1		Abandonment and collapse
2		Use inferred
3	Fl. 1	CS. 1-3; ca. 1,335 m^3

Architecture

Although details at the roof and basal levels are incomplete, Str. 5D-105 seemingly consists of three major components: building, building platform, and lower substructure (probably the supplementary platform). As noted above, construction staging does not correspond to these divisions.

Although 5D-105 is essentially horizontal rather than vertical, its substructure represents more than half (57%) of the estimated total height. As seen in frontal view (Fig. 41b), the height of the whole entity is 39% of its estimated total basal length. That is, 5D-105 is roughly a little more than three times as long as it is high, which proportionally makes it a rather high range-type structure.

The exterior building plan is rectangular without rear outsets, side insets, or lateral front extensions. Length is approximately seven times the depth because of the presence of only a single range or rooms. The central room is approximately 25% longer than the others. A difference of this magnitude emphasizes the central axis of the structure. Axial focus is also reflected in the exterior doorways. Debris profiles suggest three doorways, each centered on a room, the central opening wider than the others. Because of the difference in room lengths, the doorways define larger spaces at the center than at the building ends.

As estimated from fragments, the upper zones amounts to 76% of the wall height and thus to 43% of total building height. In Rm. 1, vault height on the other hand is only 46% of interior wall height and 29% of total room height. The increased proportional significance of upper-zone height is achieved by raising the vault spring on a course of supra-lintel masonry, a standard procedure for most late buildings covered in this report.

The building platform is suppressed to little more than a basal molding accounting for only 5% of the total structure height and 11% of the building height. Exterior walls of the building do not vary significantly in thickness; curiously, the interior walls are slightly thicker. Thickness would not seem to be an advantage for such short walls, although they are the only ones bearing double vault masses. In total the walls occupy 49% of the gross building area.

Frontality, in known features, appears in the front location of the doorways and stairway. The upper zone includes sculptural treatment in the rear, but how this relates to frontal development is not known.

Distinctive attributes of Str. 5D-105 include absence of a floor under the walls of the building; presence of hard, smooth, wall-top plaster; a vault-back surface without plaster; supra-lintel masonry; thin veneer facing stones specialized as headers and stretchers in continuous courses that extend through the walls from exterior to interior; and a stepped vault-soffit profile. Each except the latter is a feature of late buildings included in this report. Facing masonry on 5D-105 represents a high standard of workmanship as indicated by dimensional control and regularity of surface finish.

10

Structure 5E-51

Structure 5E-51 (Fig. 42–46; 67c–69) lies immediately W of Group G in the irregular line of large structures including Temple V and the South Acropolis on the southern edge of the Tikal central zone of monumental architecture. It is accessible along an overgrown path and thus is one of the least visited of the well-preserved central structures at the site—a pity because it strongly retains the romantic image of a crumbling ruin in thick, enshrouding forest.

Although not perceptible to the visitor, a plaza space extends in front of the structure, to its S, on a platform built up above the natural landform contours that descend from the elevated ground of the site center. It is obvious only on the map (TR.11) that 5E-51 is the N structure of a group in which all others are much smaller and probably not vaulted.

Structure 5E-51 itself is a vaulted, two-story "palace" or range-type structure, with forward lateral extensions at each end. It is typical of what appears to be the final period of architectural maturation at Tikal.

Maler described and named the structure "The Palace of the Rear Chambers and Giant Stone Benches" (1911:13–15; Fig. 2; 1971:39–40; Plan 15). Tozzer (1911:108–109; Pl. 29) numbered it Structure 4, which includes the adjacent Str. 5E-50. Maler's description is uncharacteristically inaccurate. The sectional drawing shows the vault soffits of the rear rooms as concave, although they are actually straight lines. The plan omits lateral extensions and includes non-existent small rooms adjacent to the transverse rooms at each end. The upper story he places behind the building instead of above the rear rooms. Maler's confusion probably resulted from the quantity of debris that engulfs this structure. He seems to have gone beyond what he

could actually see. In 1966, when it was recorded in the architectural survey, the substructure was completely obscured, the upper story had almost disappeared, and the E end had completely collapsed. The building plan (Fig. 42) could be drawn only by assuming symmetry of the E and W ends.

The lintel of Dr. 5 is partially intact. To gain access to Rm. 3 behind this doorway, a shallow trench was cut into collapse material. While sheltering from rain, the investigators cleared a pit down to floor level immediately inside of Dr. 8. In the upper story the floor of Rm. 10, initially visible at the collapse edge, was exposed back to the bench inside the room (Fig. 44a). These excavations, more ambitious than usual for the architectural survey, provided more information than was accessible to Maler.

Construction Stages

Stage 3: Substructure, Building Walls, and Vaults

There are no plaster surfaces on the wall tops or under the walls and building platform. Consequently, all these features and the substructure are included together. Vault-back surfaces mark the completion of this stage.

Debris conceals all substructural details. Presumably, there is a stair on the S side (the front) where total substructure height is between 4 and 5 m. A substructure of this height almost certainly would have two components: a building platform and a supplementary platform.

Table 32
Structure 5E-51
Facing-Stone Dimensions (m)

	Number	Mean (m)	Standard Deviation	Range (m)
Interior stretcher width	37	0.65	10.59	0.39–0.78
Interior header width	32	0.23	2.54	0.17–0.29
Interior header height	—	—	—	0.19–0.33
Vault width	—	0.27	2.32	0.21–0.36

Exterior wall faces are mostly fallen or covered with debris. A small area of wall surface emerges from detritus immediately beside the central doorway (Fig. 44c). Here the wall can be seen in section. Course levels marked by white mortar layers extend through the core from exterior to interior. The wall top consists of a similar layer of white mortar, no more substantial than a course level.

Outside wall facings are rectangular, regularly coursed, with headers and stretchers clearly distinguishable and almost equal in frequency. A representative stretcher is 0.60 m wide, 0.30 m high, 0.18 m deep; a header is 0.23 m wide, 0.32 m high, and 0.60 m deep. Although header and stretcher dimensions are essentially identical, their shapes are quite different. The headers taper in plan and section to a roughly pointed butt. Mortar joints are of medium thickness (2–6 cm) and spalls are moderately frequent (17 to the meter). Exposed surfaces had been dressed to a smooth, regular finish after construction. No plaster survived on the small areas of exterior wall surface that could be examined.

Wall core includes hard flint nodules and broken flint rubble in a dark matrix of muddy mortar. Facing stones, in contrast, are set in white, hard mortar that extends in thin lenses across the course levels through the wall (Fig. 44c).

Interior wall stretchers have a moderately high degree of variability (Table 32). Comparable statistical data were not obtained for the exterior. On both faces, headers are almost as frequent as stretchers, but in no apparent pattern. Interior masonry was smoothly finished after wall construction and covered with a single coat of hard white plaster and, as far as could be seen, no paint. Interior wall surfaces are vertical or have a slightly negative batter as in the rear wall of Rm. 1 (Fig. 43).

Floor 2 in Rm. 2 is most likely primary (Fig. 43); however, because no floors were cut through, this is not certain. Because of debris, Fl. 2 was not traced to a primary wall. The small part of it that was seen, near the center of the room, is a hard, smooth, unburned plaster.

The plan configuration of primary walls (Fig. 42) defines eight rooms of simple rectangular form, varying systematically in dimensions. Built into these walls and plastered integrally with primary wall plaster are 14 cord holders (Fig. 42: 3, 4, 7, 8, 9, 10, 13, 14, 15, 17, 18, 19, 20, 21). These vary considerably in form and detail. Some cord holders are located at doorways, others at the ends of the rooms. Cord holder 8 in Rm. 5B has the only primary ceramic insert. Cord holder 11 in Rm. 5A also has a ceramic insert, but is in a secondary partition and unrelated to no. 8. The others not only lack ceramic inserts but do not appear as though they ever had any. Paired cord holders 9, 10, 13, and 14 have vertical wood pegs, 4 and 7 have vertical bone pegs and 3 and 8 have horizontal bone pegs. The shape of the opening around the pegs varies from circular in 3, 4, 7, 8, to rectangular in 9, 10, 13, and 14. Numbers 17, 18, 19, 20, and 21 are closed by secondary plaster seals.

Primary walls contain, in addition, a number of circular holes plastered integrally with the walls, 0.10 to 0.15 m deep, and with diameters approximately equal to depths. These are shown unnumbered in Fig. 42. They are roughly at midwall height and usually do not line up in pairs across rooms or in any other obvious pattern.

In the rooms of the first range, three primary niches are visible: two in Rm. 1 (Fig. 69b, c), one in Rm. 8 and a fourth, assumed for symmetry, in Rm. 3. They are plastered integrally with the walls.

Wooden lintels survived over primary Dr. 2, 6, 7, and 14 (Fig. 43; 67c,d; 68a). The Dr. 2 lintel consists of three beams cut to form a flat soffit, with upper surfaces unmodified except for removal of bark. Butts extended about 0.76 m past the doorjambs and were hidden behind a thin plaster cover in a narrow recessed horizontal channel. Figure 67d shows this lintel recess with part of the plaster removed to expose the end of the outer beam.

The lintel of Dr. 14 consists of a larger and undetermined number of smaller unmodified beams. In this case, butts are concealed behind masonry integral and flush with the wall plastering. The Dr. 7 lintel appeared essentially identical with 14, but was even more obscured by rubble.

Rod row socket holes are present just under the lower vault spring in Rm. 1 and 8 (broken lines running into walls in Fig. 42), but appeared to be absent in the second range and in the lateral side extension. Diameters varied from 3 to 5 cm, and for 14 spaces between holes from 0.40 to 1.25 m in the two rooms. The average (mean) spacing is 0.96 m with a standard deviation of 23.14, which indicates very little preference for any one value.

A step-up in floor level from front to rear rooms is reflected in a double vault spring in the first range (Fig. 43; 44c; 45b). Apart from this distinction, vault-soffit profiles are similar in all vaults: straight-line or very shallow concave profiles with steeper end-soffits.

Figure 45b shows a section of the outer half-vaults in Rm. 1, the only accessible vault section in the building. It had obviously started to fall by spreading outward at wall-top level. The heavy broken line indicates the estimated original soffit profile, and therefore, the amount of displacement that has taken place. Soffit stones are all headers, not just in this section, but in all vaults where masonry could be examined without a plaster covering. Soffits are six course high; course heights varying from 0.24 to 0.39 m. Face widths (Table 32) have a standard deviation of 2.32 in half-vault soffits and 3.04 in end vaults; evidently the builders were more selective about masonry in the half-vaults (which do all the work) than in the short end vaults. Soffit faces had been smoothly dressed after construction and plastered with a single, thin white coat prior to installation of capstones. Because there is no appreciable pause between wall and vault construction, the entire interior except for capstones was probably plastered in one operation.

Interior surfaces of vault headers are roughly shaped, irregular, and taper sharply to a narrow butt (Fig. 44c). A good quality white mortar is tightly packed around them. This combination of stone shape and mortar quality provides the essential structural capacity of the vaults—a fact surely known to the Maya builders. Little or no vault core lies between the soffit stones and vault-back facing. The latter was evidently applied after the soffit masonry had been built up; instead of horizontal layers running through the vault core, there is a sloping mortar face just behind the headers. This marks the outer edge of the good quality, tightly packed soffit mortar. Vault-back masonry is set in a lower grade of loosely packed mortar. Vault-back facing stones had been dressed prior to installation and not smoothed afterward. No traces of vault-back plaster could be seen, other than a light gray mortar topping on the medial moldings.

Capstones had been preplastered over their entire under-surface prior to setting and, on the central axis, had been sealed in place with no less than four sequentially applied plaster layers of floorlike material (Fig. 43: U. 1, 2, 3, and 4). Possibly U. 2, 3, and 4 are grading units installed to level up the vault and subroof prior to roof and upper-zone construction. There is an absence of equivalent units over the Rm. 3 vault.

Three vault beams survived more or less intact and four butt ends remained in sockets. All beams and sockets in Fig. 46 are primary except for one socket in Rm. 5A that looked secondary. Some primary sockets are probably hidden behind the secondary partitions in Rm. 2, 5, and 6. Beam patterns are identical in Rm. 1, 2, and 8, except that the central paired beams are rectangular in Rm. 1 and 2 and round (modified) in Rm. 8. Also, Rm. 1 has a set of additional beams at the ends of the room between the two lower vault springs. Socket depths vary from 0.20 to 1.00 m with a mean value of 0.58 m and a high standard deviation of 19.8. There is no obvious pattern to the variation in socket depths at the three beam levels; hence, total beam length must have been proportional to the distance between soffits. That is, shorter beams were set at the top and longer ones at the bottom, as would be expected. The average socket depth of 0.58 m is slightly less than the thickness of the header mortar, but some beams must have protruded beyond this into the vault-back material and even into upper-zone material. There is no indication of a sequence of vault-beam installation relative to masonry. Nonrectangular beams were probably unmodified natural logs.

Stage 2: Roof and Upper Zones of the Building

Presumably, the building roof is the hard smooth plaster surface identified as Unit 1 (Fig. 43). Only a small area of this was seen, not enough on which to measure camber.

Upper-zone material has collapsed everywhere, except in one small area between Dr. 1 and 3 (Fig. 44c), and possibly where hidden beneath debris at the rear. The three or four facing stones still in place are of veneer type similar to wall stones, but thinner and with shallow relief carving on the surface. The location suggests that the carving is peripheral design between major motifs centered over doorways. No traces of plaster or paint are retained.

Stage 1: Walls, Building Platform and Vaults of the Upper Story

The south-facing upper story consists of five vaulted rooms directly over the second range of the building. Its remains are so fragmentary that a 1:100 plan did not seem warranted and thus it is shown diagrammatically (see Fig. 45a). Nevertheless, the plan configuration is reasonably clear and the locations of three cross walls are measurable.

Walls and building platform are lumped together in a single construction stage on the basis of the evidence shown in Fig. 44a. The walls rest directly on the plastered surface of U.1, which is assumed to be the roof of the building. Unit 1 shows no signs of weathering beneath upper-story material. The building platform abuts the inner face of the rear wall, indicating unexpectedly that the walls were built prior to it. Unfortunately, it is unclear whether the walls had been plastered before installation of the building platform.

All upper-story vaults and the upper parts of walls had collapsed, but numerous vault stones in debris above the level of the building roof leave no doubt that the upper story was vaulted.

Wall composition in the upper story is known for interior cross walls only (Fig. 44b). These are relatively thin walls with coursed veneer facings averaging 0.35 m high by 0.20 m thick. Additional wall surface data were not available. Core consists of quarry scrap aggregate quite unlike that of the building, but set in good quality, clean white mortar.

The primary room floor in the upper story is Fl. 5, a hard smooth plaster surface that abuts primary walls.

Presumably, the upper story was completed with upper zone and roof elements, which, if present, would constitute an additional construction stage. These features have completely fallen and cannot be recognized in the debris.

Modifications

The most substantial modifications consist of the set of partitions, U. 13, 8, 9 and 10, and 11 in Rm. 4, 5, 2, and 6, respectively (Fig. 4a). By symmetry Rm. 7 should have a corresponding partition hidden beneath rubble. The secondary partitions extend up to capstone level and have imitation vault profiles with outsets at the vault spring and near vertical faces on both sides of each unit. Secondary end-wall U. 6 and 5 (in Rm. 5 and 6, respectively) physically united with U. 8 and 11, through bench U. 19 and 23. These also have imitation vault profiles. These modifications create a

new set of rooms (4a, 4b, 5a, 5b, 2a, 2b, 2c, 6a, and 6b) by subdividing the primary rooms 4, 5, 2, and 6.

Units 19, 21, and 23 are interior platforms. They are physically integral with secondary partitions and end-wall units in Rm. 2, 5 and 6. Floor 1 is a thin skin-coat united with U. 21 over Fl. 2 in Rm. 2. All of the interior platforms associated with secondary partitions have the same form, which is a front upper molding and raised ends. On U. 23 the raised end extends across the room to the front wall.

Plaster covers the surfaces of these secondary features so extensively that masonry attributes are not observable. The standards of workmanship, smoothness of finish and evenness of line, nevertheless, appeared at least equal to those of primary elements.

Secondary partition doorways are vaulted (Fig. 43). Other integral features include niches in Rm. 2 (Fig. 43: 4) and cord holders 1, 5, 6, 11, 16, and 22 in Rm. 4a, 5a, and 2a (Fig. 42). The cord holders have fully plastered circular openings and in number 11 a ceramic insert. Number 1 has a horizontal wooden peg, 2 a vertical wooden peg, and the others have vertical bone pegs. Cord holder 2 had been installed secondarily in the primary wall of Rm. 5b, presumably with the secondary partitions. The partition surfaces contain several shallow circular plastered holes (unnumbered in Fig. 42). These are similar to those in primary partitions, and not related to other holes in any obvious pattern.

A number of other modifications to primary features may or may not represent the same round of alterations. These include the secondary sealing of primary cord holders 9, 10, 13, 14, and 15, with well-made mortar smoothly flush with wall plaster. Secondary Rm. 6b is nearly filled by U. 24 that does not reach the doorway and thus abuts primary surfaces only. The unit is low with a flat top and no moldings. Units 25 and 26 in Rm. 1 abut only primary surfaces, yet resemble the larger partition-related interior platforms in form. In Rm. 10 of the upper story, the flat-topped interior platform U. 27 overlies and abuts primary surfaces (Fig. 44a, 45a). It overwhelms the room, leaving only a small area of floor just inside the doorway (Fl. 4, a thin soft secondary skin-coat). Masonry U. 14, 15, and 16 are added to primary wall surfaces in the upper story. How these relate to the interior platforms was not discovered. Their facing stones are veneer slabs (Fig. 44b), thinner than those of primary walls; their cores consist of quarry scrap and broken flint in a good quality light gray mortar.

Some units are clearly modifications to secondary features. Interior platforms U. 18, 20, and 22 abut partitions in the small secondary rooms that they fill. They are low and have flat tops. In Rm. 6b a frontal extension, U. 12, was inserted between the U. 24 platform and the secondary partition U. 10. Cord holders 5, 6, and 16, although installed integrally in secondary partitions, were sealed later with carefully made mortar plugs smoothly finished and flush to wall surfaces.

Doorway 9 to Rm. 4b is blocked to vault-spring level by U.7. Unevenly finished with a low-grade soft plaster or mortar, this partial seal is inferior to other construction in the building.

In all modifications except U. 7, the high quality of workmanship implies changes made within the Late Classic Period.

Other Features

Burning was noted on Fl. 4 in front of U. 27 in Rm. 10 of the upper story, on Fl. 1 in front of U. 21 in Rm. 2, and on the floor in front of U. 17 in Rm. 4a. In the latter case, no appreciable area of floor surface was cleared, but a quantity of dark gray ash and several blackened stones appeared just above floor level. This material might represent a hearth, but was not in a concentrated position on the floor.

Relation to Adjacent Stratigraphy

Structure 5E-51 adjoins 5E-50, but whether it is later than this or the platform extending to the S could not be established. The other structures on the platform, 6E-5, 6, 7, and 8, look so unlike 5E-51 that a temporal difference may be suspected.

Architecture

Structure 5E-51 occupies the northern position in the group of structures (6E-1 through 18) to which it apparently belongs. All the southern structures and their platforms align to the N of magnetic E, whereas 5E-51 and 5E-50 diverge to the S of E. This could reflect different dates of construction—both in time of year and in era—or a contrast in cultural significance. The position of the central axis of 5E-51 is approximately 7 m W of the plaza center line. Such eccentricity is uncommon in structure-to-space relationships at Tikal.

Observable in nearly every feature of the structure are two general types of relationships, those that create visual unity by similarity of form, and those that express the importance of the central axis. Examples of the first (unifying) type include: (1) the repetition of building and upper-story plan with the doorways and outsets of the smaller upper story almost lining up with those of the building below; (2) primary rooms of

Table 33
Structure 5E-51: Time Spans

Time Span	Unit and Floor	Comment
1		Abandonment and collapse
2		Use inferred
3	U. 7	Sealing of Rm. 4b
4		Use as modified
5	U. 12, 18, 20, 22	Cord holder 12; sealing of cord holders 5, 6, and 16
6		Use as modified; burning on Fl. 1, Fl. 4, and in front of U. 17
7	U. 5, 6, 8–11, 13–17, 19, 21, 23–27; Fl. 1	Interior platforms; secondary partitions; 13–17, 19, 21; cord holder 2; sealing of cord holders 9, 10, 13–15
8		Use inferred
9	U. 1–4; Fl. 2, 3, 5	CS. 1–3; ca. 4400 m³ cord holders 1, 3, 4, 7, 7, 8, 11, 16–22

the same rectangular shape; and (3) the doubled vault spring in the first range that provides an upper spring at the same level as that of the second range.

The second type of relationship (focusing on axis) controls almost every element in the structure. The axial doorways are the only ones aligned vertically from the building to the upper story, centered on room spaces and aligned with their interior doorways. They are wider than the others and axial rooms are longer than other rooms. The two front non-axial doorways are pulled in toward the center, far off the centers of the rooms they access, to form a tight grouping around the central doorway and to create roughly equal wall widths. Lateral side extensions project forward far enough to form strong visual terminations to the axial composition of elements, but not so far that they become visually independent elements as in 5D-63.

The combination of lateral symmetry with front-to-rear asymmetry is carried to an extreme in 5E-51. Rear rooms are wider than front rooms, lateral side extensions project to the front only, side doorways are offset toward the front, secondary doorways into the small lateral rooms are offset toward the front, and secondary niches in the same walls toward the rear. Admittedly, the doorway positions reflect interior platform size, but the niches do not and in any case the placement of these features conforms to a general pattern from which only the cord holders are exempt. Even vault beams follow the formula of axial symmetry combined with front-to-rear asymmetry. The central axial beams are squared in axial Rm. 1 and 2, but rounded in non-axial front rooms and absent in non-axial rear rooms.

There are some remarkable subtleties in the play of dimensions that set up these relationships. The primary axial rooms in the building are 14.9% longer than adjacent rooms, but only 8.9% longer than lateral side extension rooms, greater precisely where axial contrasts are needed. Contrasting lengths between axial and transverse rooms are not so significant because with these rooms axial symmetry is expressed by frontal projection, not by room length. Rear rooms are 13.6% wider than front rooms, but only 4.6% wider than transverse lateral rooms. The greater difference occurs here where it is most directly connected with front-to-rear relationships.

The only aligned elements off the principal axis are interior platforms and the doorways that confront them. This relationship seems to have been highly valued in this edifice and was contrived at considerable expense; the secondary end-wall units seem to have no other function than to redefine interior space so that benches could be centered on doorways.

Attributes that imply a late construction date for Str. 5E-51 include large, veneer-type facing stones on both interior and exterior wall surfaces; masonry face dressing after setting of stones; thin, white plaster in one coat only; preplastered capstones; upper-zone height greater than wall height; and suppression of the building platform to little more than a basal molding. Attributes not typical of late construction at Tikal include the absence of a plaster wall top and thin walls relative to room width.

A number of features are unique or at least unusual for Tikal: vaults without springs (in secondary partitions); double vault springs (in first range rooms); vaults no thicker than the depth of the soffit headers; rectangular vault beams; doorways recessed into walls (Dr. 7, 14); and half-round lintel beams.

11

Group 5E-11, Group G

The structures that make up Gp. 5E-11 stand beside the Méndez Causeway about 100 m SE of the Central Acropolis. They form an eastward extension of a series of roughly aligned structures and groups that mark the southern edge of the central concentration of monumental architecture at Tikal. With the exception of Str. 6F-27 at the S end of the Méndez Causeway, structures and groups S of Gp. 5E-11 are no longer linked by contiguous paved plaza surfaces.

Group 5E-11 includes Str. 5E-55/68 and 6E-49/53, with at least 19 surface constructions (TR. 11) clustered around four plazas. Most of them appear only as mounds with no accessible architecture. The Tikal map (TR.11) shows only 5E-57 and 58 as standing and 5E-55 with a broken-line building component on its summit. In the architectural survey, the plan of 5E-55 can be resolved, whereas that of 5E-57 is unintelligible. Accordingly, the two structures representing Gp. 5E-11 in this report are 5E-55 and 5E-58. Maler describes and draws a plan of Str. 5E-58 (El Palacio con Fachadas Acanaladas) with parts of 5E-57 and 60 (1911:11–3, Fig. 1; 1971:38–9, Pl. 14). Tozzer presents plans of Str. 5E-50, 55, 58, and the group (1911: Fig. 18, 19; Pl. 29).

An excellent report was published on the 1972 and 1980 excavations within the group by Miguel Orrego C. and Rudi Larios V. of the Parque Nacional Tikal de Guatemala (1983) with section, plan and detail drawings of Str. 5D-55, 56, 58, 60, 61, 68, newly numbered 88 and 91, and underlying structures and platforms.

Although the present report is based only on data gathered prior to the Orrego/Larios excavations and has not incorporated their information, it nevertheless merits inclusion in the present volume, both for com-parative purposes and as complements to their far more intensive investigation.

Structure 5E-55

The largest single structure in the group, Str. 5E-55 (Figs. 47; 48) represents in volume of material one of the largest at Tikal. It forms the western side of the group and dominates the whole assemblage. Now, because it is so high, has few standing features and is covered with vegetation, one can visit 5E-58 and never even see 5E-55 nearby.

Maler makes no mention of 5E-55 but Tozzer provides a plan (1911: Fig. 18), calling it Str. 2. His drawing indicates that the fragments of wall he saw in 1910 are essentially those visible today. He assumed that the building was vaulted, yet the depth of rubble in the rooms does not seem sufficient to represent fallen vaults.

Architectural recording was done by Loten in 1969 with the assistance of Payson Sheets. The building plan (Fig. 47a) is not wholly decipherable from surface features: walls protrude above debris in only a few places and many walls are dislocated. Consequently, rectified plan lines have been used to connect visible fragments that have been left askew in solid line.

During the survey, excavations were confined to two points (Fig. 47a; 48a, b) where wall base information could be gained without cutting through much overburden. Elsewhere, recording was done at the debris line. Orrego and Larios (1983) present another plan of the building (I.A. 3), a section (I.A. 5), and discussion of architecture and dating (133-142). Their plan and profile differs slightly from ours.

Table 34
Structure 5E-55
Stretcher Dimensions (m)

	Number	Mean (m)	Standard Deviation	Range (m)
Exterior width	10	0.51	9.09	0.41–0.74
Exterior height	9	0.30	5.27	0.25–0.43
Exterior depth	6	0.23	5.21	0.15–0.31
Interior width	22	0.64	7.84	0.47–0.80
Interior height	24	0.31	3.79	0.20–0.39
Interior depth	9	0.19	2.50	0.15–0.22

Construction Stages

Only one construction stage is noticeable and includes the supplementary platform, the building platform, and the building walls.

The supplementary platform is a massive component assumed to reach entirely from the building platform down to the front plaza level. No facing masonry is visible. A horizontal strip of core masonry is exposed across the center part of the rear (Fig. 47b). A debris bulge indicates the presence of a wide outset stairway at the center of the E side. There does not appear to be a plaster floor on top of the supplementary platform under the building platform (Fig. 48b).

The core masonry exposed at the rear, about halfway up the slope (Fig. 47b), consists of large subrectangular (round-edged) blocks horizontally bedded and possibly coursed. Total supplementary platform height is approximately 7.5 m at the rear and 16.5 m at the front, the discrepancy reflecting the natural contours.

A small portion of the building platform was uncovered by clearing rubble near the SE corner (Fig. 48b). Its three courses of masonry, at a slight batter, measure 0.82 m high. Facing stones are large thin veneer slabs, face dressed after installation and set in thin mortar joints with no spalls. There are no floor surfaces running either under the building platform or walls.

The building walls stand, at most, four courses (ca. 1.20 m) high. The uppermost surviving blocks project, for the most part, a few centimeters above the nearly level debris that fills the rooms. Wall facings consist of large thin veneer slabs, consistently coursed but apparently all stretchers, at least in the visible areas of wall surface (see Table 34). Values of standard deviation are high indicating that dimensional standardization is moderate. Interior facings are similar. A greater number can be seen; their average dimensions are slightly larger on the face and less in depth. Visible face surfaces were dressed after installation, but are badly distorted by partial collapse, deterioration of core masonry, and tree-root action.

There is no floor under the walls of the building (Fig. 48a). The single interior floor has a topping of 8 cm pebble aggregate in dark gray mortar turning up to the primary walls.

The walls cannot be seen clearly enough to determine the room pattern unequivocally. Figure 47a therefore is an estimate. Some rooms appear to be unusually wide (more than 4 m) and nearly square, whereas others are long and narrow, more or less normal. Because the rubble is only about 1 m deep and does not include many large blocks of stone, it does not look like vault material, even though the walls are thick enough to have supported vaults. In some places, building walls are unaccountably thick (up to 4 m) at structurally inconsequential places, yet the accumulation around them is no greater than elsewhere and apparently they did not support vaulting.

A total of 14 chambers seem to be defined by the primary walls. The pattern is so irregular, however, that unrecognized modifications may have occurred. It is also possible that some of the apparently secondary walls are in fact primary, and that unseen walls exist beneath debris. Figure 47a also shows 19 doorways; however, there is no certainty that all are in fact primary. All doorway widths (except Dr. 1) are drawn 2 m wide, based on an estimate from Dr. 10.

It seems likely that the edifice had a beam and mortar roof. In the small excavation at C-C' (Fig. 48b), the debris overlying the floor consisted almost entirely of light, fine-grained material with few large stones.

Modifications

The secondary partitions indicated in Fig. 47a are based on cursory examination without exposure of wall bases. The abutments might be sequences within primary construction.

Relation to Adjacent Stratigraphy

Although Str. 5E-55 seems externally to be integral with the cluster formed by 5E-56, 57, 58, 60, and 61, stratigraphic controls are not yet available (see Orrego and Larios 1983).

Architecture

Structure 5E-55 is one of the larger works of architecture at Tikal. Its supplementary platform is nearly 17 m high at the front and 70 to 75 m long, and the building is approximately 57 m long.

The combination of high substructure and long, multi-chambered building brings together attributes that are normally either on temples or range-type structures. Other instances of this combination at Tikal (none with a substructure as high as this one) are on portal structures providing entrance to plaza spaces (e.g., Str. 5E-1). Structure 5E-55 is distinctly not a portal, however, as no rear stairway can be distinguished on the W side.

The difference noted earlier between front and rear of the supplementary platform heights indicates that the structure was built over a slope with its rear on higher ground (Fig. 47b). As a result, if the rear had an estimated three terraces, the front would have around seven. The lower four would have to terminate somehow on the ends, perhaps by abutting flanking structures.

Even though the edifice seems to be unvaulted, it may have the "I-"shaped exterior plan configuration common in vaulted range-type structures at Tikal. The primary room arrangement appears to be two ranges in the center part and three transverse ones in the lateral side extensions. In three central sections, the room pattern consists of a narrow chamber in front of an extraordinarily wide one. The reverse is found in one section (Rm. 3 and 7). Although the exterior doorway placement is symmetrical, it does not seem to have been followed by a similar symmetrical room arrangement. The secondary partitions divide the square rooms in two and create a more standard three-range effect.

The front and rear faces of the building, each with five doorways between the lateral side extensions, are essentially identical—a relatively rare instance in a structure with no rear stairway.

Circulation from the front of the building to the N lateral side extension seems to have been possible both initially and after the addition of secondary partitions, but not to the S end. This asymmetry might indicate different functions at the two ends of the building.

Table 35
Structure 5E-55: Time Spans

Time Span	Unit and Floor	Comment
1		Abandonment and collapse
2		Use inferred
3		Seconday partitions
4		Use inferred
5	Fl. 1	CS. 1; ca. 15,800 m^3

The apparent absence of vaulting on an edifice of this size, so closely linked to other large vaulted buildings, seems peculiar, especially when the walls were thick enough to carry vaults. Possibly the structure was never completed, as Orrego and Larios conclude from the thick walls, lack of vault stones, and lack of interior platforms (1938:136). The presence of interior plaster and secondary walls imply, on the other hand, that it was not only completed, but endured long enough to undergo alterations. The wide primary rooms 1, 3, 8, 9, and 10 do not look like spaces that were ever intended to be stone vaulted, but could have been spanned by thatch or beam and mortar. Perhaps the heavy walls expressed only the importance of the building.

Architectural attributes indicating chronology are few. A late construction date is suggested by the absence of a floor running under the walls of the building, the relatively small size and simple shape of the building platform, and the large, thin, veneer wall-facing stones surface-dressed after installation.

Structure 5E-58

Structure 5E-58 (Figs. 49–53; 69d–72) is notable as the first large, well-preserved work of architecture seen by Maler when he arrived at the site in 1895 (1911: Fig. 1; 1971: Pl. 14). He named it the "Palace of the Facades with Vertical Grooves," and saw it as a quadrangle enclosing a courtyard. When the Tikal Project mapped the area (TR.11), two sides of the quadrangle were seen as separate constructions with 5E-58 occupying the E and N sides and undoubtedly forming the front to the whole group.

The building is an enormous, single story range-type structure with lateral side extensions that give its front a powerful formality. It possesses the unusual feature of a vaulted, curving tunnel that provides a kind of secret passage into the inner courtyard from the E side through a large grotesque mask. It was recorded by

Table 36
Structure 5E-58
Facing-Stone Dimensions (m)

	Number	Mean (m)	Standard Deviation	Range (m)
Exterior stretcher width	—	0.56	3.36	0.47–0.64
Exterior stretcher depth	—	0.20	—	—
Vault height	—	0.30	3.53	0.26–0.36

Hug in 1964 and by Loten in 1966 as part of the survey of standing architecture. At that time, debris obscured most of the rooms and the entire substructure. Subsequently, Guatemalan archaeologists of the Parque Nacional excavated extensively, finding earlier constructions and much new detail, recently publishing an excellent account of their discoveries (Orrego and Larios 1983).

The asymmetrical "L"-shaped plan clearly faces E. A set of axial doorways in the E wing and a second entry system through the center of the N wing provided access to the courtyard through the building. On the roof, above the N and S ends of the building and extending over Str. 5E-57 as well are roof structures that appear to be upper-story components. These could be secondary additions, but in the absence of clear evidence they have been included as parts of the original 5E-58.

Construction Stages

Stage 5: Supplementary Platform and Building Platform

These two components, which constitute the whole substructure, are clearly marked as a separate construction stage by a plaster surface, Fl. 2, that runs under the building wall in Rm. 11 (Fig. 52a). At this point on the W side of the building, the platform is about 1 m high and on the northern side grades from approximately 3.5 m to a maximum height 7 m. Facings on the E side have eroded away. A wide stair is reconstructed here, but no stair bulge showed in debris.

Two room levels exist in the building, a lower one for rooms in the E, or front façade, including the lateral side extensions, and a higher level for rooms facing the courtyard. Floor 2 implies that the platform was entirely finished and plastered prior to erection of the walls.

The tunnel, shown in Fig. 49a, 52b, and 53, is entirely within the substructure at its northern entry, but rises to emerge in the courtyard with its capstones and vault above room floor level. The northern entry is in the center of a large carved deep-relief mask, apparently representing a face with the tunnel as the mouth (Fig. 53). The sculpture was finished with a single coat of thin white plaster retaining no traces of paint. The tunnel vault consists of two courses set back from the wall surface to form a recessed spring (Fig. 52b).

Stage 4: Building Walls

The walls were erected over the hard, smooth plaster of Fl. 2 (Fig. 52a) that apparently functioned as the primary room floor after construction. Wall heights are constant at around 3.0 m, although not measurable in many places. Thicknesses vary greatly; the E (front) wall, for example, is thinner than the W one. Short walls between rooms in the front range are highly variable in thickness (perhaps reflecting room measurement near the wall top). Corresponding walls in the courtyard range, on the other hand, appear more consistent and decidedly thicker. The medial wall in the eastern wing is much thicker than any other in the building. Maler mistakenly thought that it must have therefore supported a second story. Finally, the northern wing might be a secondary addition.

Wall faces are vertical where not distorted by structural failure or root invasion. Both interior and exterior surfaces had been smoothed and dressed after construction. A single coat of hard, thin, white plaster covers both surfaces and the wall top.

Exterior wall surfaces have vertical grooves about 10 cm wide and deep, spaced an average of 0.85 m apart. A sample of 15 spaces between grooves on different parts of the exterior ranged from 0.75 to 0.98 m. The grooves had been cut into the masonry after construction and before plastering. They retain traces of red paint that had probably covered the whole outer wall.

Exterior masonry is consistently coursed with an average course height of 0.35 m. Mortar joints are thin (ca.

2 cm) and spalls are almost completely absent. Facing stones (Table 36), predominantly stretcher widths, have a standard deviation of 3.36, indicating high control of dimensions. They are about 0.20 m in depth, roughly shaped on all surfaces and smoothed on the exposed face after setting. Interior facings are similar.

Core masonry consists of quarry scrap in a tight dark mortar. The walls had not collapsed sufficiently to provide adequate sectional data indicating whether course levels passed through the wall cores.

The 22 rooms within the building manifest non-random dimensional variations. Rooms 1, 2, and 3 on the E-wall axis exceed all others in length; Rm. 2 and 3 are considerably narrower. Both dimensions emphasize the importance of the central axis as well as the tendency to have wider rooms in the front. The narrowness of Rm. 2 and 3 may reflect a desire for a temple-like three-room design on the central axis in a building otherwise two rooms wide. Rooms 14 and 17, the central passage rooms of the N wing, are much shorter than others in the same wing. This again relates to a through-passage, but here, in a subsidiary entranceway, the rooms are made shorter rather than longer. Rooms in the courtyard range of the N wing (13 and 15) are wider than Rm. 16 and 18 behind them, suggesting that the wing faced the courtyard rather than outward as the E wing. Reversal can be noted in the lengths of non-axial rooms of the E wing. In the front range, the shorter rooms (5 and 21) are remote from the axis, whereas in the rear range they (Rm. 9 and 10) are adjacent to it. Perhaps the intention was to impart a contrasting frontality to the facades—the one as front to the whole group and the other as front to the courtyard.

Similar inverse patterns were developed in doorway placements. To accomplish this the doorways were placed eccentrically in the non-axial rooms in such a way that the front wall lengths adjacent to the axis are less than the remote ones, whereas in the courtyard this relationship is reversed. Exterior doorways in the E wing appear to be the widest (but could not be measured directly).

No primary subspring beams or cord holders were noted in the building, although some of those listed further on as modifications may have been original.

Stage 3: Lintels, Vaults, and Medial Corbels

After wall construction, wooden lintels were placed over doorways on plastered lintel beds approximately 0.50 m below the levels of the wall tops. Only one exterior lintel, that over Dr. 12, has survived even in part (Fig. 52a). It appears to have been made up of 10 uncarved logwood beams averaging approximately 0.10 m in diameter, with butts extending 0.85 to 0.90 m beyond the doorjambs. A better preserved lintel with 12 similar beams remains in place over interior Dr. 21 (Fig. 71c). Butt ends had been concealed behind masonry housings plastered flush with the wall surface.

Supra-lintel masonry was installed over the wooden beams to provide an even bedding for the vaults. In the case of Dr. 12 (Fig. 52a), a mortar line is observable at the top, indicating a minor pause between supra-lintel and vault masonry not of sufficient duration to constitute a construction stage.

The next operation was the placement of the first vault header course and (at the same time) the medial corbels that form the lower part of the exterior medial molding (Fig. 52a). Mortar and core material in which these headers and corbels are bedded extends unbroken across the wall top. The corbels average approximately 0.80 m in depth and vary from 0.40 to 0.50 m in width. Heights average 0.30 m. The stones are triangular in plan shape, tapering sharply to a pointed butt. On their top surface is a thick coat of very hard plaster that is probably the base of a vault-back surface, even though no other trace of vault-back plaster was seen.

Vault masses were temporarily finished with a coursed vault-back facing of roughly squared stones set on edge, like thin veneer slab facings (Fig. 52a). These average 0.50 to 0.60 m wide by 0.30 m high and approximately 0.12 m deep. No vault-back plaster remained on the exposed facings (but these were not examined where plaster might have been protected). Cores were built up in tilted course levels, with dark mortar that contrasts with the white mortar employed in the facings (Fig. 71d). At each course level, the white mortar runs back from the facing into the core.

Vault stones consist almost entirely of sharply tapered headers. They are quite variable in shape (Fig. 52a), an attribute that may reflect use of vault stones from a demolished structure. Soffits are uniformly six courses high, with course heights ranging from 0.26 to 0.36 m around a mean value of 0.30 m and a standard deviation as low as that obtained for wall facing stretcher lengths (Table 36). Soffit headers are nearly all square on the face. Much smaller stones appear at the top course, presumably to create a level capstone bed.

Soffit surfaces had been dressed and smoothed to a straight-line profile after vault construction on both transverse and end-vault elements. A single coat of thin white plaster had been applied prior to the setting of the capstones, but survives only where it turned out onto the capstone bed (not visible in Fig. 52a).

Elsewhere, over the whole building, vault-soffit plaster has completely vanished, probably as a result of hydraulic pressure caused by water in the vault mass. This in turn reflects the absence of a protective upper story and deterioration or possible absence of vault-back plaster.

Capstones, as seen from within the rooms, are side tapered and their joints form a diagonal dovetail pattern between the vault soffits. Perhaps they were quarried as either soffit headers or medial corbels—the two stone types generally sharply tapered—but then were not used in these locations, particularly in vaults, because other material became available through demolition. The underside had been dressed and plastered prior to installation, the plaster covering two-thirds of each stone. There was no indication that the diagonal joints had ever been concealed by additional mortar or plaster.

Capstone plaster is the only such surface to survive inside the rooms above wall-top level. Evidently it was of superior quality (perhaps sun-cured before installation).

Vault-spring levels are set at the two different wall-top levels corresponding to floor levels and constant in each room. The ratio of vault height to wall height is 1:1.57 (that is, walls are slightly more than one and a half times as high as the vaults). Walls and vaults together create rooms approximately 5 m high with an average width-to-height ratio of 1:2.86 (that is, heights are nearly three times the width).

No vault beams have survived and because of loss of soffit plaste;, beam shapes are not clearly indicated. Better preserved socket holes with rounded or oval shapes suggest logwood. Beam patterns were recorded in Rm. 11, 8, 20, 19, 6, 12, and 15, but are not illustrated here. The central ranges of the E wing have a three-level beam pattern whereas all others, including those in the lateral extensions, have only two levels. Diameters vary only from 0.10 to 0.13 m. Butt lengths for middle level beams (n = 4) are much more variable and in no apparent order. Those of upper level beams (n = 17) range from 0.39 to 1.15 m with a mean value of 0.57 m and a standard deviation of 28.9, indicating a scattered distribution with little preferred value. Butt lengths for middle level beams (n = 4) range from 0.55 to 0.92 m, have a mean value of 0.72 m, and a standard deviation of 14.2. The lower-level beams (n = 21) range from 0.35 to 1.54 m, have a mean of 0.70 m, and a standard deviation of 27.7. Even though the lower level provides more room for variation, they are slightly less variable than upper level beams. Of all the beam sockets measured, only one at upper level passed right through the vault mass.

Stage 2: Roof and Upper Zone

No surface survived in roof areas accessible without excavation. A front-to-rear step-up is reconstructed in Fig. 51, reflecting the known step-up in medial corbel levels. It would have fallen with the outer vaults of the front range.

Upper-zone facings have fallen everywhere except for a few fragments in the courtyard façade. These suggest a complex lower profile perhaps with no real medial molding (Fig. 52a). Essentially the same profile appears on the lateral side extensions (Fig. 71a). Under Façade Sculpture 1 (Fig. 52c; 69d), the medial molding is closer to the usual form.

Medial corbels occupy two different levels in the building. A lower level extends across the E façade, both lateral side extensions, and through the S wing into the courtyard, where it ends against the building wall just below the medial corbels of the W façade (Fig. 70c).

Upper-zone remains were not sufficient to allow reconstruction of the complete profile (Fig. 51; 51) or corner treatment. No plaster or paint survives. The full height had to be deduced from estimated roof levels and appears to be nearly equivalent to the height of the walls.

The mask element in the SE courtyard corner (Façade Sculpture 1; Fig. 52c) is the only upper-zone sculpture still in place. It is not clear that a fully sculptured upper zone can be inferred from this because the few surviving details seem quite unlike other upper-zone elements on the building. The mask is carved in deep relief and finished with thin plaster that is largely eroded away. Broken stones indicate a projecting "nose" element. There are no traces of paint.

Stage 1: Roof Structures

Because little is known about the roof structures, they have been combined with the roof as a single construction stage. They consist of U. 1 and 2 over the N and S wings (Fig. 49b). The southern unit extends W over Str. 5E-57. Only fragments of both remained, and even these were obscured in rubble. From the great deal of debris that accumulated against the base of the N and S wings, it is assumed that U.1 and 2 represent substantial features such as the upper stories shown in Fig. 49b. Visible masonry is of the thin veneer type, smoothly finished and consistent with other facing masonry of the building. No obvious stairway could be located.

Table 37
Structure 5E-58
Radiocarbon Dates

	Vault Beam 1 (Lab no. P-964)	Vault Beam 3 (Lab no. P-965)
5568 half-life	A. D. 675 ± 47	A. D. 376 + 41
5730 half-life	A. D. 636 ± 48	A. D. 375 + 42
*MASCA calibration	A. D. 690 ± 50	A. D. 450 + 40
RIC calibration	A. D. 610 - 880	A. D. 385 - 610

*(Klein 1982)

Modifications

Assuming that the N wing is truly primary, secondary elements of the structure are limited to interior platforms (benches), refloorings, subspring beams, and cord holders.

Four interior platforms were seen (Fig. 49a), and rooms shown without benches might also contain them. The assumption that the benches are secondary is based on U. 3 in Rm. 11 (Fig. 52a), which rests on the primary room floor and abuts primary wall plaster. Units 3 and 4 are room-filling benches with a single top level. In association with U. 3 is Fl.1, laid over the small open space in front of the doorway. This floor had been heavily burned over its whole surface. Facing stones of U. 3 are similar to those of the building walls, but less carefully dressed and set in hard, muddy mortar of inferior quality. No plaster remained on top and front surfaces.

Units 5 and 6 in Rm. 6 are also assumed to be secondary. These are end-room, two-level platforms (only the rear upper level can be seen in Fig. 71d). Facing stones show a somewhat higher standard of workmanship then on U. 3.

Subspring beams had been installed in Rm. 6 by breaking through primary wall plaster. Because the holes align with the front edges of the benches, it is assumed that the two features are related in time. Diameters range from 5 to 10 cm. The N socket of beam 1 (Fig. 49a:8) retains a removal scar (Fig. 71d), where beams had been repeatedly removed and inserted.

A small hole in the N jamb of Dr. 12 (Fig. 52a:14) indicates the installation of a beam through primary plaster.

The one cord holder recorded is to the N of the Rm. 11 doorway on the exterior wall. It had a vertical wooden peg but no ceramic inset. A hole had been cut into original plaster to receive the peg and the mortar that held it in place.

Other Features

No graffiti were noted. Floor 1 had been heavily burned over the whole area in front of the bench in Rm. 11, but the collapse debris on the floor did not cover charcoal or other occupation material.

Relation to Adjacent Stratigraphy

Structure 5E-58 abuts against 5E-57 and perhaps 5E-61. The sequence of abutment is not clear.

Architecture

Structure 5E-58 is an "L-"shaped, range-type edifice with a two-component substructure, doorway openings in both principal facades, lateral side extensions, roof structures, and aligned doorway openings that provide passage through the principal axis and the N wing.

Fragmentary remains of the roof structures suggest that they may be upper-story elements placed on both ends of the building. The lateral side extensions project frontally only. Although 5E-58 is physically connected with other structures on its W façade, the E façade has the appearance of a freestanding architectural entity and therefore was probably the front. Doorways in both facades are eccentric to their rooms and thus seem to relate to the exteriors rather than to the interior spaces. Thus as with Str. 5E-1, both may have been regarded as fronts, one to the group as a whole, the other to the courtyard space. As described above, the facades exhibit inverse relationships in terms of room dimensions and doorway spacings that imply contrasting architectural design.

The aligned E axial doorways (1, 8, 9, and 10) suggest that at least part of the functional program of 5E-58 may have been a provision for formal entry to the group. These doorways can be seen as a monumental portal system fully integrated with the building. The vaults step up from E to W, reflecting ingress in this direction. The existence of a relatively broad, architecturally defined plaza to the E of the building further supports the inference of formal entrance from this side. Aligned Dr. 14, 18, and 17 imply a second formal entry system through the N wing, less formal perhaps, from a smaller courtyard, and apparently without the step-up in vaults. Existence of the tunnel indicates an even less formal (or service) entryway to the courtyard.

The doorway spacing, the axial entry, the lateral side extensions in one façade only, and the vertical grooves suggest a concern for exterior form independent from room arrangements. Seventeen of the 22 rooms are accessible directly from the outside; 13 do not lead to other rooms. Except for Rm. 12, 19, and 20, all interior chambers are only entered through aligned doorways linked directly to outward space. This limited interior circulation suggests that exterior form was essential to its functioning as a front to both the group and the courtyard.

Most architectural attributes predicate a late date of construction. These comprise dimensionally standardized, thin veneer wall facings on both interior and exterior surfaces; preplastered capstones; plastered wall tops; masonry surfaces dressed after installation; walls and upper zones of nearly equal heights; and finally, the large scale of the structure. Earlier attributes are a plastered floor under walls of the building, and, perhaps, red paint on exterior wall surfaces.

Absolute Dates

Two samples of wood cut from vault beams were subjected to radiocarbon testing in 1965. They were taken from Rm. 1, Beams 1 and 3, still in place within the original N soffit sockets. Samples from the outer under-surfaces of the beams were identified as *Piscidia Piscipula* (*Habín* in Spanish). The results of testing by the University of Pennsylvania MASCA laboratory were returned in 1965 (Satterthwaite and Coe 1968:12) and revised in 1982 to conform to new half-life and calibration formulae.

The RIC range includes both the statistical and the calibration uncertainties (Klein et al., 1982). Reuse might account for the discrepancy between the two beams as had been suggested for a comparably early vault beam in Temple I (Coe and Satterthwaite 1968:8). The later date range is more likely, placing the building in the 7th to 9th centuries or the "Late Classic."

Table 38
Structure 5E-58: Time Spans

Time Span	Unit and Floor	Comment
1		Abandonment and collapse
2		Use inferred
3	U. 3–6; Fl. 1	Interior platforms
4		Use inferred
5	U. 1, 2; Fl. 2	CS. 1-5; ca. 7,730 m^3

12

Group 6B-2

Group 6B-2, also known as the Barringer Group, is an isolated architectural assemblage located approximately 1 km SW of Great Temple IV (TR. 11, Perdido sheet). The cluster includes the short Morley Causeway and approximately 25 structures, 6B-16 to 37. Structures 6B-26 and 37 form a quadrangle on a group platform and define a plaza containing stela P42 and three uninvestigated chultuns.

Most of the units are fully mounded over but two, 6B-24 and 6B-33, have long rear walls standing clear of debris. Unfortunately, 6B-24 has collapsed to the extent that the room plan cannot be determined without excavation and is not included in the survey. Although 6B-30 and 36 initially appear less well preserved than either of the two "standing" structures, they provide sufficient information for a plan drawing and therefore have been included. Recording was done in 1969 by Loten and Sheets.

Structure 6B-30

Occupying the E side of the quadrangle and sustained by the principal platform, 6B-30 (Fig. 54–56) faces W into the plaza. The rear wall stands to medial-molding height at the center. Both side walls have fallen; the single room, the front of the building, and the entire substructure are concealed beneath rubble deep enough to suggest a fallen roofcomb.

Construction Stages

Stage 3: Walls, Building Platform, and Supplementary Platfom

There is no visible horizontal surface running under either the walls of the building, or the building platform.

Therefore, the entire substructure and the walls are included together in CS. 3, terminated by wall-top plaster.

The only visible supplementary platform masonry is a narrow layer of core material exposed at the rear of the structure (Fig. 55:2), its top suggested by a noticeable change in the character of core masonry. The supplementary platform core body is made of uncoursed, medium-sized stones, horizontally bedded in thin mortar.

No facing masonry of the supplementary platform remains exposed. A bulge in rubble on the W side probably indicates an outset stairway. Two terraces as shown in Fig. 55 are conjectural.

Coursed core masonry immediately above the material just described presumably represents a building platform, the facings of which have eroded away. Layers of gray mortar mark the course levels and stone aggregate within course levels is smaller and less consistently bedded. A step-up at the base of the interior wall (Fig. 55) implies more than one level.

The back wall of the building rests on the raised rear part of the building platform. Exterior wall stones are rectangular blocks approximately 0.22 m thick, consistently coursed, and specialized as headers and stretchers. Header frequency is approximately one to every two stretchers. Although course levels run continuously through the standing part of the wall, heights and widths vary considerably (Table 39). Surfaces were dressed after installation. Mortar joints are moderately thin and devoid of spalls. Course levels of white mortar run through the wall core from exterior to interior between the darker bands of core mortar. No exterior plaster remains.

From the rubble pattern and a few protruding edges, it appears that the walls define a single room

Table 39
Structure 6B-30
Facing-Stone Dimensions (m)

	Number	Mean (m)	Standard Deviation	Range (m)
Exterior wall width	12	0.52	7.03	0.33–0.59
Exterior wall height	12	0.37	5.66	0.31–0.54

approximately 1 m wide with one front doorway. The room floor was seen as a plaster-turn at the interior wall-foot, but could not be examined further without excavating. There appears to be only one floor present. On this surface at the N debris edge lies a solitary stone dressed and plastered on at least three sides. This may be the fallen and broken arm of an interior platform (Fig. 54:1; 55:3).

Stage 2: Vaulting

Vaults are preserved to over half the original height. Soffit details are not visible without excavation, although it seems likely that features exist beneath debris. The rear half-vault was built along with the exterior medial corbels and has a plastered vault back (Fig. 55). Soffit stones and one preplastered capstone are sufficiently specialized to be recognized amid the fallen material. The former are sharply tapered, approximately 0.60 m deep and at maximum 0.32 wide. Surfaces appear to have been dressed after installation.

Stage 1: Roof and Upper Zone

The only remaining upper-zone material is a small amount of core masonry that still adheres to the plastered vault back (Fig. 55). No facings remain in place. From the amount of debris present it seems likely that the structure had a roofcomb.

Relation to Adjacent Stratigraphy

Nothing is known about the stratigraphic relationship between Str. 6B-30 and the others on the platform.

Architecture

Characterization of 6B-30 as a "temple" is based on relative height and square proportions. The dimensions in Fig. 54 and 55 provide a height-to-width ration of 1:1.43 or 70% (without a roofcomb). The substructure accounts for 62% of the total height. In plan proportions, the building width is 2.4 times the depth (i.e.,

depth equals 42% of width). In Fig. 54, it has been assumed that similar proportions govern the substructure without the stair, making it rectangular rather than square. With the stair projection, the depth become 86% of the width and approaches a square.

The plan configuration of the building as shown in Fig. 54 and 56 is that of a simple rectangle with a rear axial outset, one room, and a single front doorway. The building platform has a higher back part sustaining the rear wall. This suggests a two-part building with a front either longer or shorter than the rear and an exterior form not corresponding to the single-room interior plan. Side-insets are also implied by the rear outset of the building. Yet side-insets of normal depth should have established an inherently stable formation that does not collapse down to floor level as has happened here.

Technical attributes of chronological significance include absence of floors under the walls of the building and under the building platform; presence of wall-top plaster and a plastered vault back; coursed wall facings specialized as headers and stretchers; specialized vault headers sharply tapered; face dressing after installation of masonry; and exterior configuration independent of interior plan.

Associated Monuments

On the axis in front (W) of 6B-30 is St. P42, the upper half of a plain stela of parallel sides and flat front (TR. 33B). The area was not excavated in search of a stela pit or the lower half of the original stone. Immediately W of this stela and more of less on the axis are two chultuns. A third is slightly farther away and a little off-line to the N.

Table 40
Structure 6B-30: Time Spans

Time Span	Unit and Floor	Comment
1		Abandonment and collapse
2		Use inferred
3		CS. 1-3; ca. 1,011 m^3

Table 41
Structure 6B-33
Facing-Stone Dimensions (m)

	Number	Mean (m)	Standard Deviation	Range (m)
Exterior stretcher width	28	0.53	6.58	0.40–0.64
Exterior stretcher height	28	0.39	2.49	0.34–0.43
Exterior header width	15	0.19	2.16	0.17–0.24
Exterior header height	15	0.36	3.61	0.27–0.43

Structure 6B-33

Structure 6B-33 (Figs. 57–59a) fills the S side of the Gp. 6B-2 quadrangle. It is the largest structure in the group in terms of volume of material (except for the group platform), and faces the Morley Causeway.

The rear wall stands clear of accumulation to full height along most of its length. Some upper-zone material is still in place in the rear. Because the rooms are filled with debris, doorways have to be estimated from rubble contours. Debris entirely conceals the substructure. Recording of 6B-33 was done by Loten and Sheets in 1969.

Construction Stages

Stage 4: Supplementary Platform

The top of the supplementary platform is a white mortar layer that runs under the building platform (Fig. 57 and 58). The rear rests on unlevelled ground and the front is at a slightly higher plaza level.

No facing masonry survives above debris. Core masonry, where visible, is tightly packed, horizontally bedded, uncoursed rubble set in good quality, tight, dark gray mortar.

Debris contours suggest a wide N stairway inset within the forward projection of lateral side extensions (Fig. 59a:2). Evidently, the plan configuration of the supplementary platform follows that of the building. The top of the supplementary platform is lower in the central division of the building than in the lateral extensions. The step-up between the two divisions seems to exist only in the supplementary platform.

Stage 3: Building Platform and Walls

There is no evidence of a plaster surface between the building platform and the walls, consequently the two are included together in one construction stage. Wall-top plaster (Figs. 57, 58) marks a pause after completion.

The building platform appears to have two base levels and a single top level. At the lateral side extension it is 0.65 m high and in the center 0.85 m high. These two heights probably compensate for the step-up in the supplementary platform and bring all rooms to a common floor level.

Building platform facings do not survive above debris. The only visible building platform material is a strip of core immediately below the exterior rear wall face. In composition, this masonry resembles the wall core.

The walls stand full-height across most of the back, but have fallen at both ends and the front. Interior walls are visible as ridges on the debris mound with occasional small exposures of facing masonry. Facings remain only at a couple of places in the rear façade. They are consistently coursed, rectangular veneer stones, specialized as headers and stretchers, one header for approximately every two stretchers in no apparent pattern. Walls are six courses high with an average (mean) course height of 0.36 m, yet with considerable height variation within and between courses (Table 41). Where facing stones had peeled away, many of the impressions in the mortar distinctly indicate turtle-backed shapes. White mortar course-levels extend through the darker core mortar from exterior to interior. Inside facings are similar to those on the outside.

Wall stones were dressed after installation to a straight-line profile with exterior walls at a slight batter. Mortar joints are thin and spalls absent. Visible facings do not retain any traces of plaster.

A series of scaffolding holes 0.10 to 0.15 m in diameter are visible across the base of the rear wall, spaced somewhat regularly with some gaps (Fig. 59a). One upper hole can be seen near mid-wall height, offset approximately 0.10 m from a lower hole. In other parts of the rear wall, particularly where facings have peeled off, there are so many bird and insect holes that scaffolding holes cannot be identified without climbing a ladder and probing each one.

The walls define a total of nine rooms: two in each of the lateral side extensions, and five in the single-ranged central part. Doorways cannot be measured directly, but their existence is indicated by depressions in debris. They presumably had wooden lintels, all fallen now with the possible exception of Dr. 4. A floor level can be identified, but no floor data are accessible. Similarly, nothing is known of cord holders, benches, graffiti, pits, burning or occupational debris.

Table 42
Structure 6B-33: Time Spans

Time Span	Unit and Floor	Comment
1		Abandonment and collapse
2		Use inferred
3		CS. 1–4; ca. 3,600 m^3

Stage 2: Vaults

The vaults rest on the plastered wall top and can be isolated as a construction stage separate from the roof because of the presence of a plaster vault-back surface (Fig. 58). Although no vault stands to full height, the bottom two or three courses survive over most of the building.

In the E lateral side extension, a small excavation exposed the largest section of extant soffit masonry. Here, four soffit courses remain in situ apparently representing about half the original vault. The spring, outset approximately 8 cm, is one course above the wall top, on a supra-lintel course level with the sharply tapered corbels of the exterior medial molding. These average 0.40 m in width at the face and taper to an almost pointed butt. Vault-back plaster turns out onto their tops to form the foot of the vault back.

Soffit stones are consistently coursed headers in half vaults and are stretchers approximately 0.60 m wide in the one observable end-vault (Fig. 58). Headers are approximately 0.30 m in height and width and 0.60 m in depth. The bedding planes of headers are not horizontal; top and bed surfaces are not parallel. Interior surfaces are roughly dressed to form a sharply tapered butt and face surfaces were dressed after installation. One stone appears to have been quarried as a header and installed as a stretcher. This suggests that pieces were roughed out at the quarry and then dressed at the construction site.

Vaults are possibly eight courses in height (ca. 3 m). This relatively high vault, nearly all of which has now

fallen, would account for the large amount of building debris.

The vault-back facing consists of small stones, about 5 cm high, horizontally bedded, not coursed and not facially dressed. Its plaster is hard and rough. Vault springs and medial moldings maintain a constant level in the center and ends of the building. Nothing is known about capstones, vault beams, or soffit plaster.

Stage 1: Roof and Upper Zones

Patches of upper-zone material survive at various points in the rear façade. The upper zone appears to extend around the building at a single level. A medial molding is observable at the rear and presumably was present at the front also. On the principal axis (Fig. 57), a few carved stones remain above the molding, but not enough to indicate the motif represented. No trace of plaster or paint appears on the facing masonry. No part of the roof or upper element of he upper zone survives.

Presence of a roof structure is debatable. Debris quantity seems suspiciously great, but this may reflect vault height.

Architecture

Structure 6B-33 is a long, single-storied entity with a central range of rooms and double transverse ranges at its ends (Fig. 59a). It is "I-"shaped in plan, the side extensions projecting to the front and rear. This shape is followed in both the building platform and the supplementary platform.

Each of the central five rooms has its own doorway. The axial chamber (Rm. 1) is 18% longer than adjacent ones, but less than 12% longer than the outer two. Doorway positions in Fig. 59a assume that they are central to the rooms.

Frontality is unequivocally expressed by an absence of openings in the rear wall and by a lesser projection of the lateral side extensions.

Late architectural attributes include no floor under the building walls; plastered wall-top and vault-back surface; thin veneer wall-facing stones, facings dressed after installation; presence of a supra-lintel course between wall top and vault spring; specialized shape of vault-soffit headers; vaults and upper zones relatively high in relation to walls; and upper-zone decoration carved into the facing stones rather than modeled in stucco. The only attribute slightly inconsistent with the foregoing is the relatively great front projection of the lateral side extensions.

Table 43
Structure 6B-36
Wall and Vault Stone Dimensions (m)

	Number	Mean (m)	Standard Deviation	Range (m)
Wall stretchers width	32	0.50	4.71	0.37–0.57
Wall stretcher height	32	0.37	2.57	0.29–0.43
Wall header width	12	0.19	2.93	0.15–0.27
Wall header height	12	0.36	2.97	0.32–0.42
Vault header width	5	0.29	2.53	0.27–0.33
Vault header height	5	0.34	2.87	0.29–0.37

Structure 6B-36

Structure 6B-36 (Fig. 59b–60), flanked by structures 6B-35 and 6B-37, defines the W side of the Gp. 6B-2 quadrangle. Less well preserved than 30 and 33, with only about half the length of the rear wall standing, this architectural entity nevertheless presents almost as many visible features. Toward its N end the rear wall has fallen, but the walls between chambers still stand and some interior details are visible. All vaults have fallen, leaving end-vault fragments in some places. Rooms are filled to wall-top level with rubble and the substructure is completely covered by debris. Recording for the architectural survey was done by Loten and Sheets in 1969.

Construction Stages

Stage 3: Walls, Building Platform, and Supplementary Platform

There is no plaster surface under walls or the building platform, hence, the walls are included together with the whole substructure in a single construction stage. Completion of CS. 3 is marked by wall-top plaster.

The supplementary platform is visible as a strip of core material just below the building platform (Fig. 60a). It is approximately 1 m high and therefore probably has only one terrace. A stair bulge occupies almost the entire E side of the platform. Core masonry consists of small stones 0.05 to 0.10 m high, tightly packed together in a good quality, adhesive, dark mortar.

The building platform is recognizable at various points across the back, where its surface has eroded away, and at the S end of the building where it was preserved beneath a shallow cover of rubble. It is two courses high, projects 0.10 m from the wall face, and has a slight batter. Surface dressing appears to have been done after setting, probably at the same time as the wall.

The walls stand full height across roughly half of the rear of the building as well as at the S end (Fig. 60b). Standing interior walls are observable in the N half, whereas only debris ridges appear in the S half of the building.

Exterior wall facings consist of thin veneer stones, approximately 0.17 m thick, squared on the face, consistently coursed, and specialized in shape as headers and stretchers. Header frequency is approximately 1 to 2.4 stretchers with no obvious header pattern. Face dimensions vary as in Table 43. Variation in height is large within any single course; in a sample of 16 stones in one course, heights range from 0.33 to 0.41 m. Because of this weak standardization, some stones had to be notched to fit the irregularities in bed joints. Some end-joints are diagonal and again adjacent stones had to be specially shaped to fit. Mortar joints vary from thin to thick. Spalls are absent. Face surfaces were dressed after installation to a smooth, vertical, straight-line profile. No interior facings are visible, and no plaster survives on the exposed exterior. A floor level can be identified, but floor data are not accessible without excavation.

Stage 2: Vaulting

The plastered vault-back surface (Figs. 60a, b) indicates that the vaults were fashioned as a separate building stage from the roof. No vault unit survives intact. The largest section still standing, to three-quarter full height, is an end vault on the S end of the building (Fig. 60b).

Springs are outset approximately 8 cm above a course of supra-lintel masonry. The medial corbel stones, shaped to a triangular form in plan, average 0.40 m wide and approximately 0.75 m deep. The vault-back plaster turns out onto their tops.

Soffit facings consist of headers in the long vaults and stretchers in the end vaults. Headers are nearly square on the face with heights slightly exceeding widths (see Table 43). Depths are approximately 0.60 m. The butts are tapered so mortar joints are thin at the face, but quickly become thicker toward the butt. By projecting the surviving soffit angles upward it is possible to estimate a total height of four courses.

At the one accessible end vault, soffit facing stones are all thin veneer stretchers essentially identical with wall-facing stretchers. The end-vault overhang is noticeably less than that of the long-vault units. All soffits appear to have been face-dressed after installation. No plaster remains on accessible surfaces.

The vault back is formed by a masonry facing of horizontal stones approximately 0.10 to 0.15 m in thickness, roughly dressed on the face. The plaster covering is hard, but not smooth and undulates over the masonry.

Stage 1: Roof and Upper Zone

Only a very small amount of upper-zone material remains in situ (Fig. 60a). A single course survives over the medial corbels near the center of the rear façade. It is set back about 0.10 m from the corbels to produce a medial molding one course high (0.25 m). Nothing survives to document the top of the upper zones or the roof. The extant facing includes no carved stones and no plaster. The full height is estimated from the vault reconstruction. The amount of debris in the rooms and around the building does not indicate any construction on top of the roof.

Modifications

At the N end of the building (Rm. 4), the posterior wall has fallen away leaving a negative rubble caste on the line of the interior wall face. Visible on this surface is U.1, an interior platform built against the primary wall plaster in the center of the room (Fig. 59b). It is the type with vertical extensions ("arms") at both ends. If similar features are present in other chambers they are completely concealed by the standing back wall and rubble that fills the rooms.

Table 44
Structure 6B-36: Time Spans

Time Span	Unit and Floor	Comment
1		Abandonment and collapse
2		Use inferred
3	U. 1	Interior platform in Rm. 4
4		Use inferred
5		CS. 1-3; ca. 1,200 m^3

Relation to Adjacent Stratigraphy

From its position 6B-36 would appear to be roughly contemporary with the structures on the same platform. Stratigraphic data are not available. Surface appearances suggest that 6B-36 predates the two smaller entities that flank it to N and S.

Architecture

A low building platform and a supplementary platform sustain the one-story, range-type structure. Its building contains a single range of five rooms, all facing E, without transverse rooms or lateral side extensions. The central room is much longer than the others and may have had more than one doorway. Debris indentations indicate a single doorway in each of the four nonaxial rooms, but do not permit precise measurement or location.

Architectural attributes are all typical of late construction: a low, almost minimal building platform; thin veneer wall stones; no floor under the walls; a plastered wall top and vault back; end-vault stretchers; a supra-lintel course below the vault spring; and face dressing of masonry surfaces after installation. Masonry dimensions are only moderately standardized, an early attribute.

13

Chronological Conclusions

The architectural sample in TR. 23A consists of only 22 structures out of approximately 500 examined by the Tikal Project. It is not appropriate to draw firm conclusions from this sample alone. Nevertheless, in describing each structure it seemed proper to identify the attributes that can be expected to establish "early," "middle," and "late" complexes in the full analysis of Tikal architectural data (TR. 34).

Features of late construction in the TR. 23A sample include plastered wall-tops; preplastered capstones; specialized vault headers; stretchers in end-vault soffits; thin white one-coat plaster; masonry surfaces finished after installation; smooth straight-line profiles; equally well-finished interior and exterior wall surfaces; veneer wall-facing stones; continuous through-wall coursing; specialized headers and stretchers; upper zones approximately as high as walls; walls relatively thick in comparison with room widths; low building platforms; low subapron elements in relation to apron heights; and supra-lintel masonry above wall tops. Structure 4D-14, 4E-47, 5E-1, 5C-9, 5C-13, 5D-105, 5E-55, 6B-30, 6B-33 and 6B-36 have consistently late attributes with no anomalous early features. They appear to be the best candidates from the TR. 23A sample for the delineation of a late architectural complex at Tikal.

The tentative "late" complex reflects a more highly organized approach to the managerial aspects of construction than was followed by the earlier builders at Tikal. There are more construction stages than in early work and they do not always correspond to the major visual components of a completed structure. Late building platforms, for example, are simple, low entities, visually separate but constructionally integrated with the walls of the building. This appears to be a con-

sistent late diagnostic at Tikal although exceptions can be seen even in the limited sample represented by TR. 23A, for example, in Str. 5E-58.

Early attributes include floors under walls; small wall-facing stones; inset panels in exterior walls; capstones not preplastered; no wall-top plaster; wall-facing stones not dressed after installation with post-dressing on substructure components, but not on the building; low vaults in relation to walls; long narrow rooms; thin walls in comparison with room width; unspecialized vault masonry; red paint; and relatively deep projection of lateral front extensions. These features are tentatively identified as "early" only in relation to others as "late" without any more precise chronological implications.

The structures representing a consistent set of early attributes in the TR. 23A sample are those on the south Acropolis (Gp. 5D-14): Str. 5D-100, 101, 102, 103, 104, and 141. They will probably belong to a "middle" complex when the analysis of chronological variation is accomplished for all of Tikal. The distinctive features of even earlier Tikal architecture, such as flat slab vaults, and small, unshaped wall-facing stones are lacking, whereas late features such as large wall-facing stones and low subaprons are present.

Structures 3D-40-43 present a mixture of early and late features, probably a deliberate archaism. The wall-facing stones in these building are small, like early facings, but are shaped to precise rectangular forms in a late manner and are as dimensionally standardized as any late wall. Vaulting in these buildings follows fully developed late techniques and does not suggest an early innovative experimentation.

The following inconsistencies can be seen in the TR. 32A sample: Str. 3D-38 and 5E-51 have large veneer wall-facing stones with early unplastered wall tops. The latter also has early thin walls relative to room widths. Structure 5E-58, with the late traits of thick walls, specialized vault stones, and veneer wall-facings, displays the early features of floors under walls and red paint on exterior wall surfaces.

The end-vault soffit stretchers of Str. 4E-47, 6B-33, and 7B-36 unite these widely separated and dissimilar buildings. This unusual treatment of vault soffits suggests the work of an individual builder and points to an understanding of structural behavior not widely held at Tikal.

Arguing against interpretation of these three works as the signature of a single builder, however, is the relatively weak dimensional standardization of wall-facing stones in Str. 6B-36, which indicate an earlier date of construction.

It is to be anticipated that a detailed comparative analysis of these and the other buildings from Tikal will establish a finer grained seriation, a better basis for inference of function, and a framework for consideration of spatial variation and iconographic interpretation. These are subjects best treated in TR. 34, the synthetic volume on the architecture of Tikal.

References

Coe, William R.
1990   *Excavations in the Great Plaza, North Terrace and North Acropolis of Tikal.* Tikal Report 14.
        University Museum Publications, Philadelphia, PA.

Klein, J., et al.
1982   Calibration of Radiocarbon Dated Tables Based on the Consensus Data of the Workshop on Calibrating
        the Radiocarbon Time Scales. *Radiocarbon* 24:103-50.

Maler, Teobert
1911   Explorations in the Department of Petén, Guatemala, Tikal: Report of Explorations for the Museum.
        Memoirs of the Peabody Museum of Archaeology and Ethnology, Harvard University 5 (1):3-91.

1971   Bauten der Maya aufgenommen in den Jahren 1886 bis 1905 und beschrieben van Teobert Maler. In
        Monumenta Americana. 4th ed. Edited by Gerdt Kutscher. Ibero-amerikanschen Institut. Gebt.
        Mann Verlag, Berlin.

Morley, Sylvanus Griswold
1937-1938 *The Inscriptions of Peten.* Carnegie Institution of Washington 435, Washington D.C.

Orrego C., Miguel, and Rudi Larios V.
1983   *Tikal Peten: Reporte de las investigaciones arqueologicas en el Grupo 5E-11.* Instituto de
        antropologia e historia de Guatemala. Parque Nacional Tikal, Guatemala.

Satterthwaite, Linton
1943   Introduction. *Piedras Negras Archaeology: Architecture I* (1). University Museum Publications,
        Philadelphia.

Satterthwaite, Linton, and William R. Coe
1968   The Maya-Christian Calendrical Correlation and the Archaeology of the Peten. *Thirty-seventh
        International Congress of Americanists* (Mar del Plata) 3:3-21.

Shook, Edwin M.
1951   Investigaciones arqueológicos en las ruinas de Tikal, Departamento de El Petén, Guatemala.
        Antropologia e Historia de Guatemala 3 (1):9-32.

Tikal Reports

TR. 5:   Shook, Edwin M., and William R. Coe
                1961
                Tikal: Numeration, Terminology, and Objectives. University Museum Publications, Philadelphia.

TR. 11:   Carr, R. F., and J. E. Hazard
                1961
                Map of the Ruins of Tikal, El Peten, Guatemala. University Museum Publications, Philadelphia.

TR. 12:   Coe, William R., and W. A. Haviland
                1982
                Introduction to the Archaeology of Tikal, Guatemala. University Museum Publications, Philadelphia.

TR. 14:   Coe, William R.
                1990
                Excavations in the Great Plaza, North Terrace and North Acropolis of Tikal, Vols 1-V.
                University Museum Publications, Philadelphia.

TR. 18:   Jones, Christopher
                n.d.
                Excavations of the Twin-Pyramid Groups of Tikal. University Museum Publications, Philadelphia.

TR. 31:   Trik, Helen W., and Michael E. Kampen
                1983
                The Graffiti of Tikal. University Museum Publications, Philadelphia.

TR. 33A: Jones, Christopher, and Linton Satterthwaite
                1982
                The Monuments and Inscriptions of Tikal: The Carved Monuments. University Museum
                Publications, Philadelphia.

Tozzer, Alfred M
1911   A Preliminary Study of the Prehistoric Ruins of Tikal, Guatemala. *Memoirs of the Peabody Museum of
                Archaeology and Ethnology, Harvard University* 17:2.

Illustrations

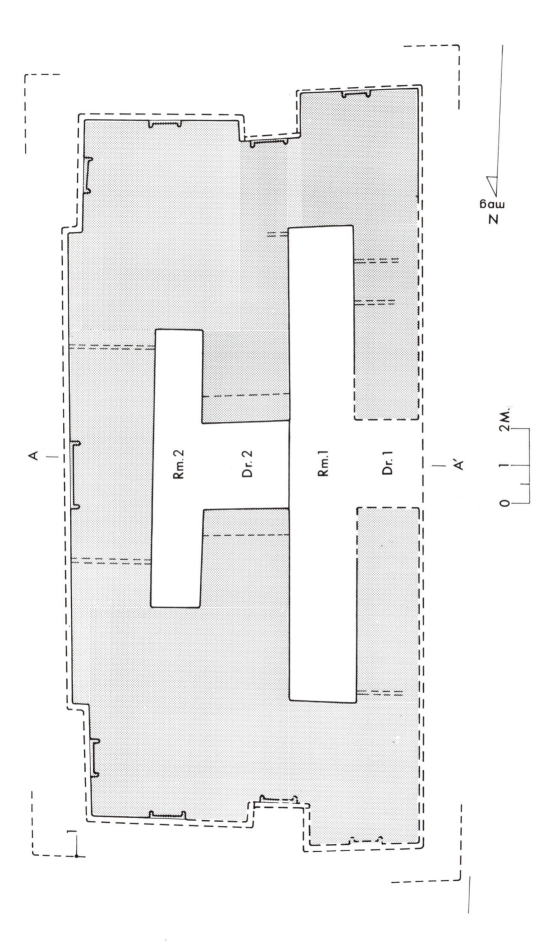

Figure 1. Structure 3D-40, Plan 1:100. 1. top of supplementary platform.

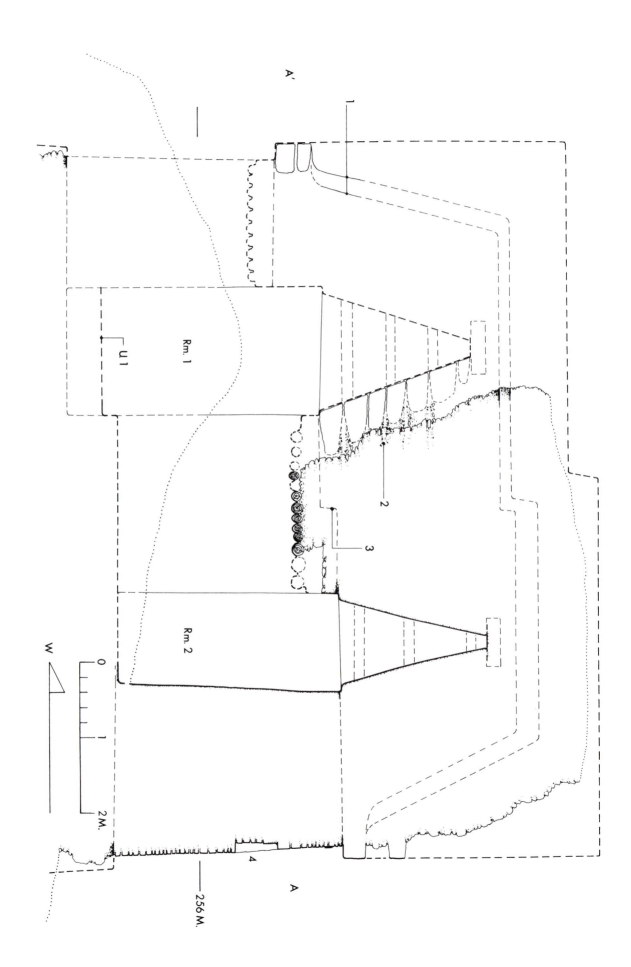

Figure 2. Structure 3D-40, Section/Profile A-A' 1:50. 1. double plastered vault back (off section). 2. course levels in vault core. 3. assumed step in plastered wall top (off section). 4. inset wall panel.

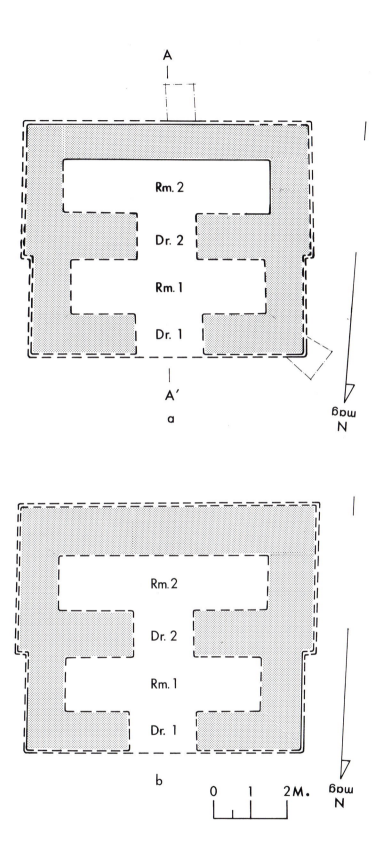

Figure 3. a. Structure 3D-41, Plan 1:100. b. Structure 3D-42, Plan 1:100.

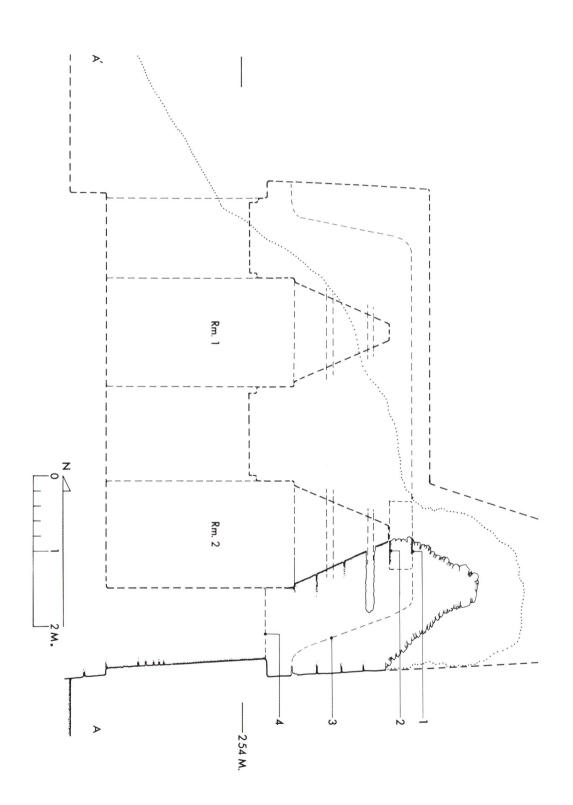

Figure 4. Structure 3D-41, Section/Profile A-A' 1:50. 1. plaster on top of capstone. 2. preplastered capstones. 3. plastered vault back. 4. plastered wall top.

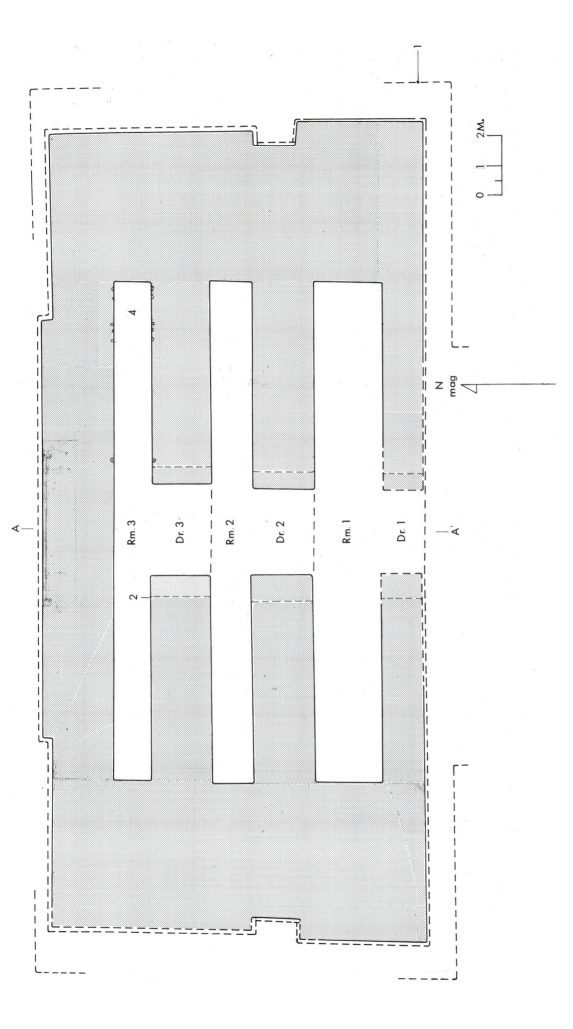

Figure 5. Structure 3D-43 Plan. Increase size 125% to achieve standard Tikal scale of 1:100. 1. estimated top of supplementary platform. 2. lintel beds. 3. inset panel in upper zone.

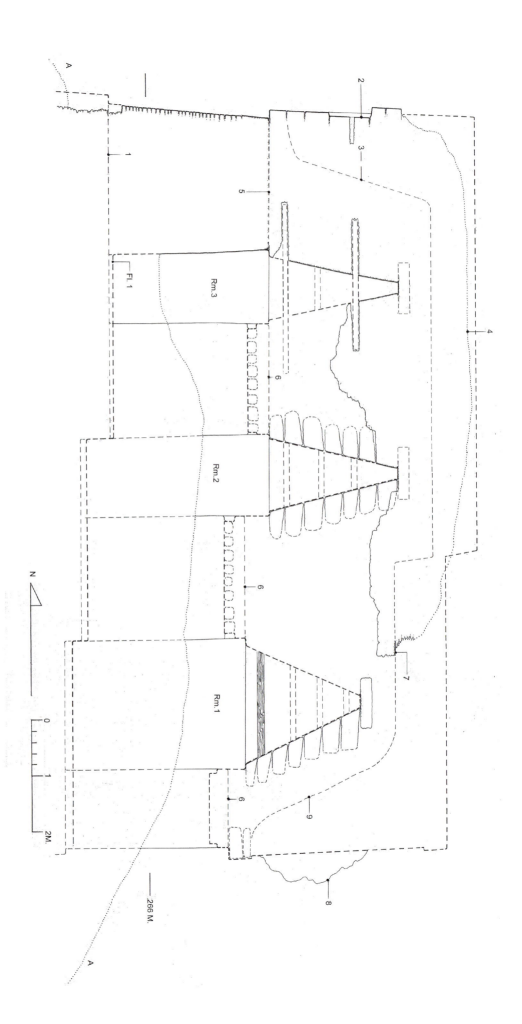

Figure 6. Structure 3D-43, Section/Profile A-A'. Increase size 133% to achieve standard Tikal scale of 1:50. 1. top of building platform. 2. mask panel. 3. plastered vault back. 4. humus level. 5. plastered wall top. 6. assumed level of plastered wall top (off section). 7. plastered subroof. 8. façade sculpture. 9. assumed line of plastered vault back.

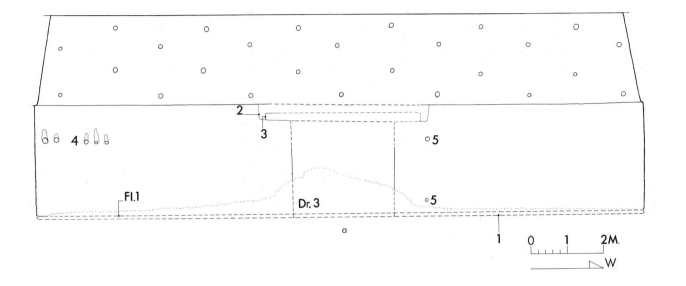

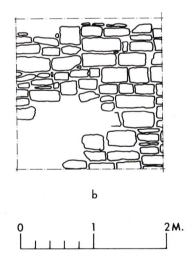

Figure 7. Structure 3D-43. a. South Elevation of Room 3 1:100. 1. assumed primary floor level. 2. plastered end of lintel bed. 3. plastered beam impression. 4. beam removal scars. 5. cord holders. b. Exterior Wall Facing 1:50.

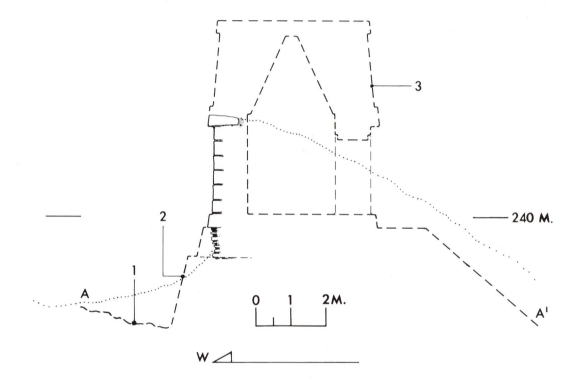

Figure 8. Structure 3D-38, Section/Profile A-A' 1:100. 1. natural grade. 2. substructure profile. 3. upper-zone profile.

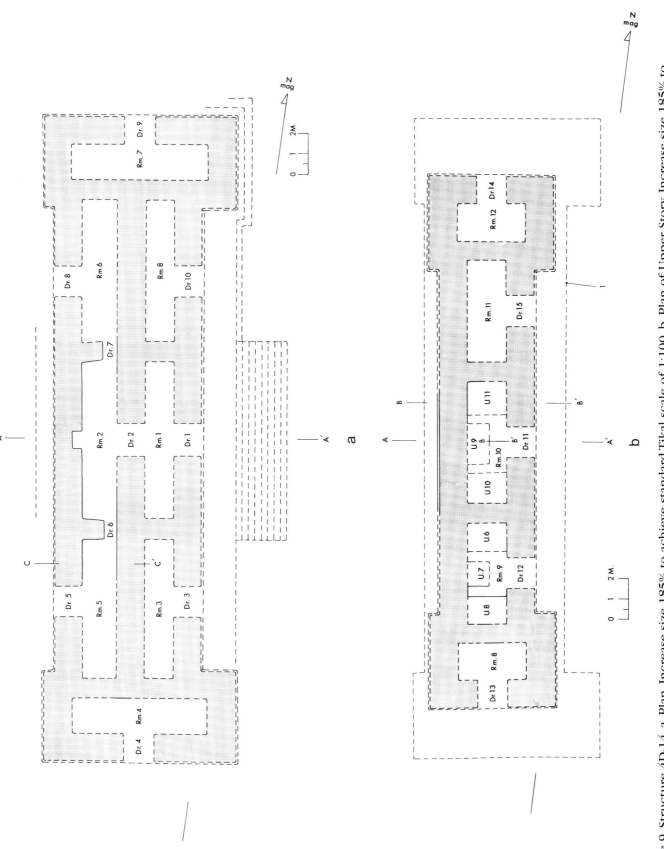

Figure 9. Structure 4D-14. a. Plan. Increase size 185% to achieve standard Tikal scale of 1:100. b. Plan of Upper Story. Increase size 185% to achieve standard Tikal scale of 1:100. 1. line of building roof.

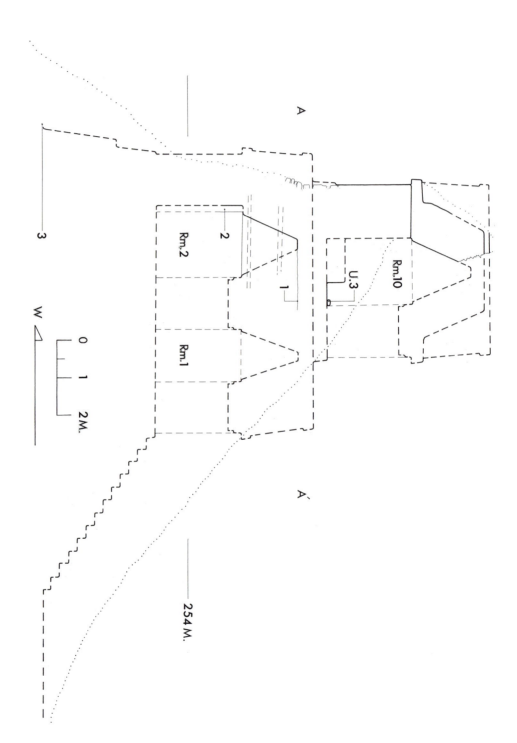

Figure 10. Structure 4D-14, Section/Profile A-A' 1:100. 1. top of double vault mass. 2. niche 3. assumed base level.

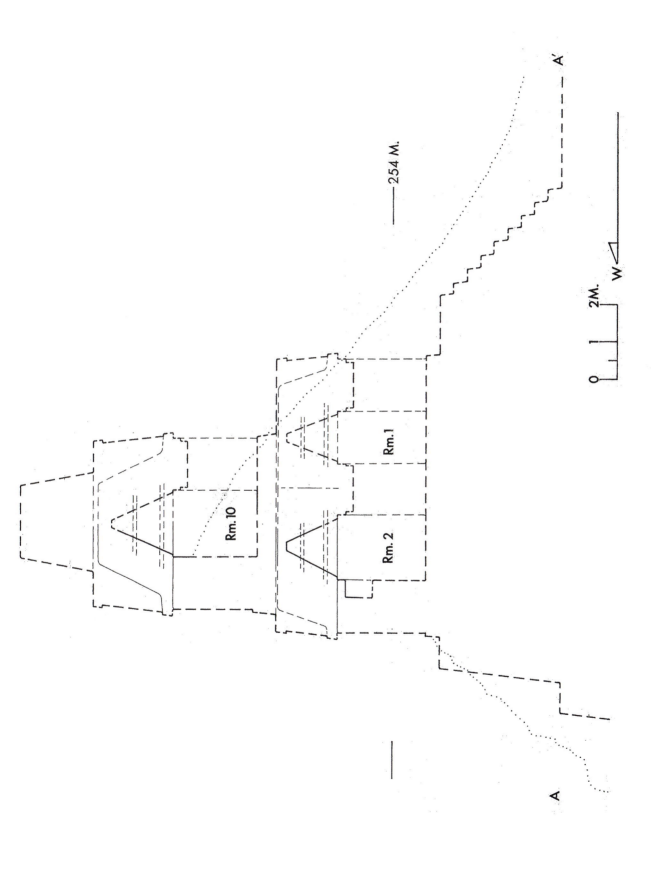

Figure 11. Structure 4D-14, Alternative Section/Profile A-A' 1:100.

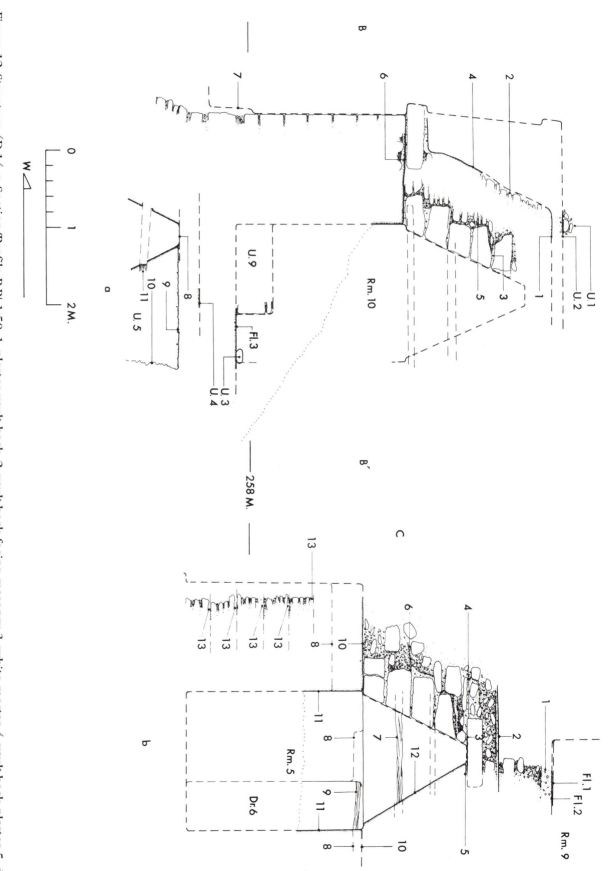

Figure 12. Structure 4D-14. a. Section/Profile B-B' 1:50. 1. plaster vault back. 2. vault-back facing masonry. 3. white mortar. 4. vault-back plaster. 5. dark mortar. 6. plastered wall top. 7. upper-story platform. 8. preplastered capstone. 9. mortar topping on double vault mass. 10. vault-back surface. 11. vault-beam stump. b. Section/Profile C-C' 1:50. 1. floor ballast. 2. hard plaster (U. 4). 3. preplastered capstone. 4. mortar topping on vault core. 5. vault soffit plaster turns onto mortar layer. 6. course level in vault core. 7. vault beam. 8. level of lintel bed. 9. lintel beam. 10. plastered wall top. 11. wall plaster. 12. vault soffit plaster. 13. white mortar layers extending through core at course levels.

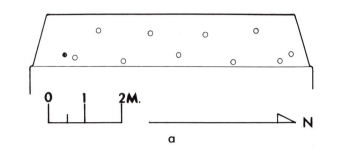

0　1　2M.

N

a

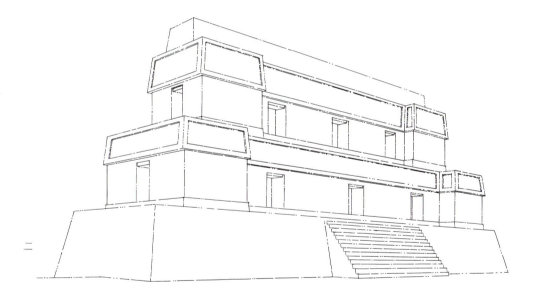

b

Figure 13. Structure 4D-14. a. Vault Beam Pattern Room 2 1:100. b. Perspective Reconstruction.

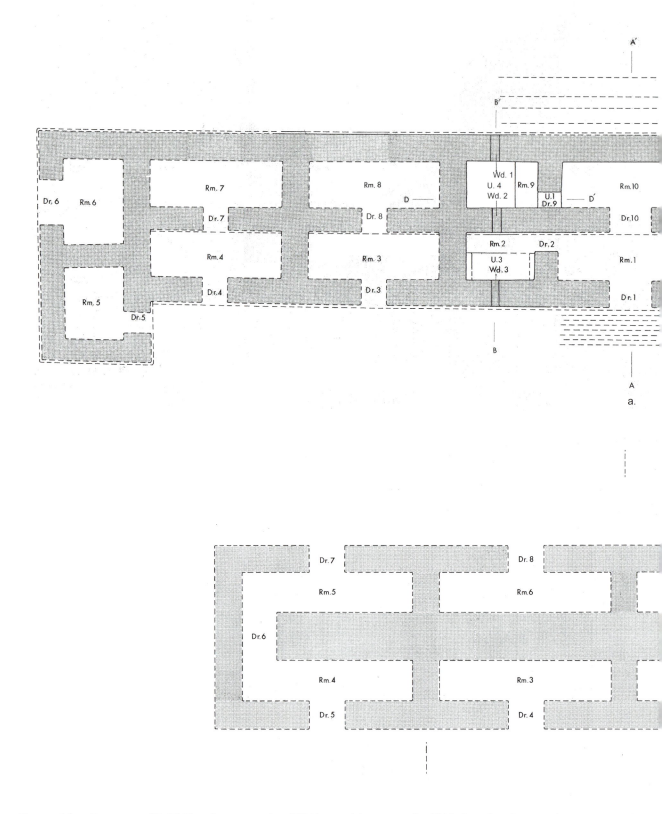

Figure 14. a. Structure 4E-47 Plan. Increase size 188% to achieve standard Tikal scale of 1:100. b. Structure 5E-1 Plan. Increase size 188% to achieve standard Tikal scale of 1:100. 1. stair side. 2. base level corner.

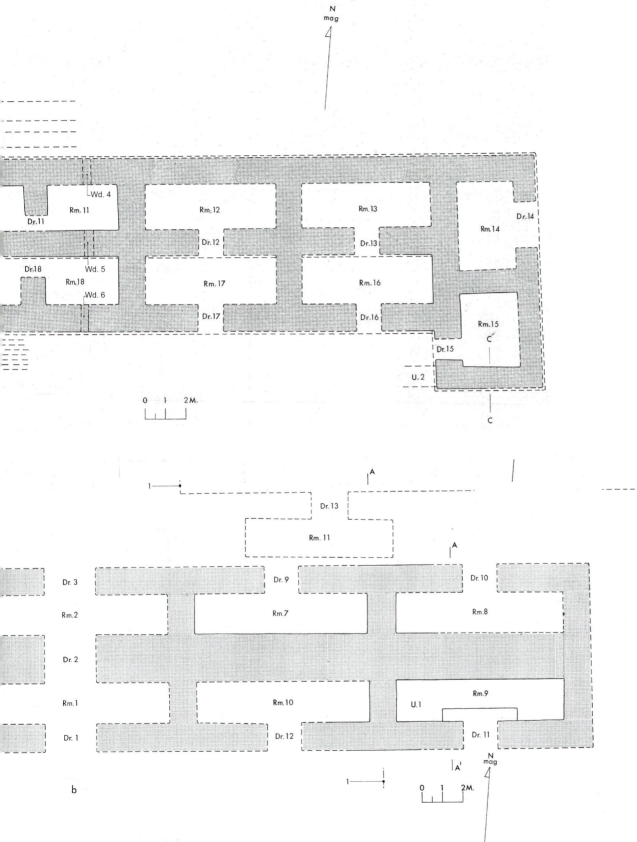

N
mag

Wd. 4
Rm. 11
Dr. 11
Rm. 12
Dr. 12
Rm. 13
Dr. 13
Rm. 14
Dr. 14

Dr. 18
Wd. 5
Rm. 18
Wd. 6
Rm. 17
Dr. 17
Rm. 16
Dr. 16
Rm. 15
C
Dr. 15
U. 2
C

0   1   2 M.

A
1
Dr. 13
Rm. 11
A
2

Dr. 3
Dr. 9
Dr. 10
Rm. 2
Rm. 7
Rm. 8
Dr. 2
Rm. 1
Rm. 10
U. 1
Rm. 9
Dr. 1
Dr. 12
Dr. 11
A'
N
mag
1
b
0   1   2 M.

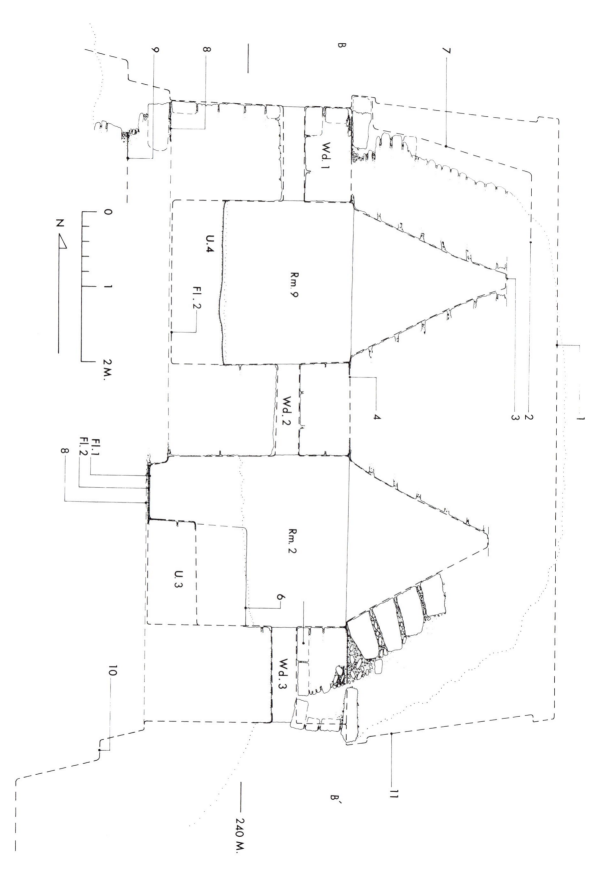

Figure 15. Structure 4E-47 Section Profile B-B' 1:50. 1. approximate level of roof. 2. assumed subroof. 3. preplastered capstone. 4. plastered wall top. 5. stone lintel. 6. raised end of interior platform. 7. vault back. 8. top of building platform. 9. top of supplementary platform. 10. assumed profile of supplementary platform. 11. assumed upper-zone profile.

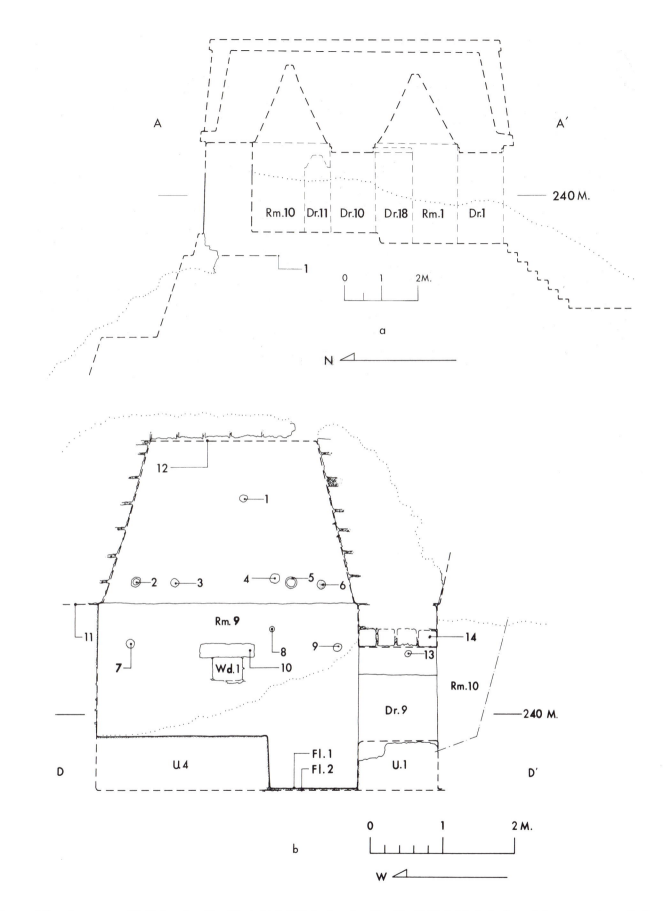

Figure 16. a. Structure 4E-47 Section/Profile A-A' 1:100. b. Section/Profile D-D' 1:50. 1, 3, 4. vault beam sockets. 2, 5. stone plugs in beam. 6. plugged and plastered socket. 7, 9. subspring beam sockets. 10. stone lintel. 11. plastered wall top. 12. preplastered capstones. 13. beam socket in doorway vault. 14. doorway vault capstones.

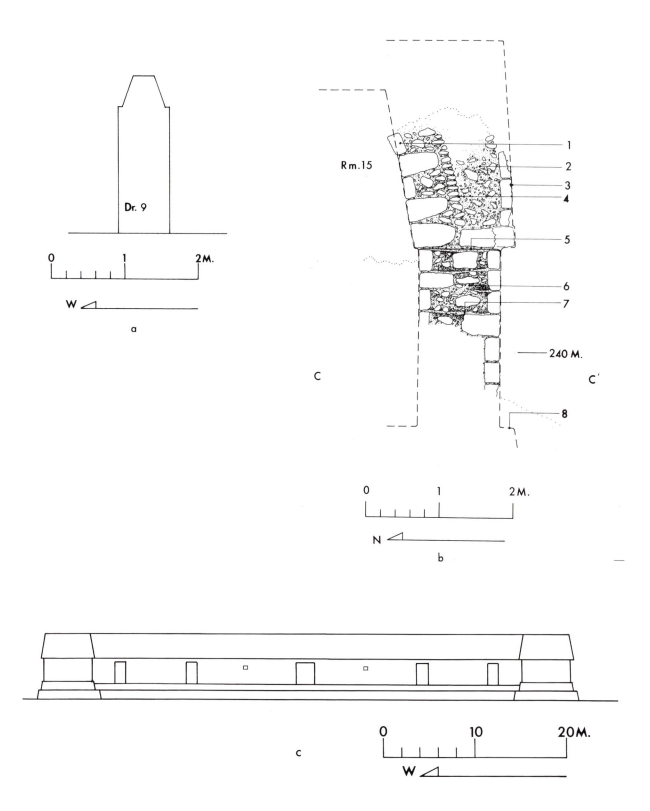

Figure 17. Structure 4E-47. a. Elevation of Doorway 9 1:50. b. Section/Profile C-C'. 1. stretcher in end-vault soffit. 2. upper-zone core. 3. carved upper-zone facing. 4. vault back. 5. plastered wall top. 6. dark wall core mortar. 7. white facing mortar. 8. top of building platform. c. Schematic South Elevation 1:400.

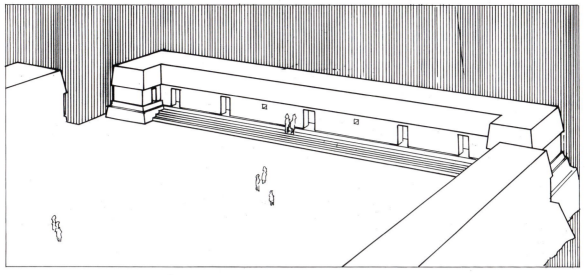

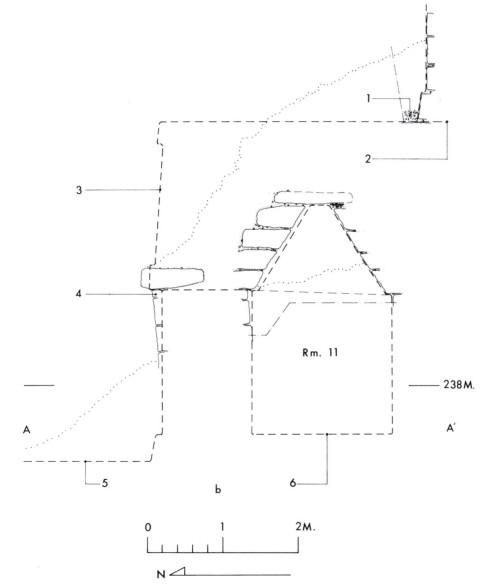

a

b

1

2

3

4

5

6

Rm. 11

238M.

A

A'

0   1   2M.

N

Figure 18. a. Structure 4E-47. Perspective Reconstruction. b. Structure 5E-1 Section/Profile A-A' (lower part) 1:50. 1. ash deposit. 2. supplementary platform. 3. reconstructed upper-zone profile. 4. wall face displaced outward. 5. estimated plaza floor level. 6. estimated room floor level.

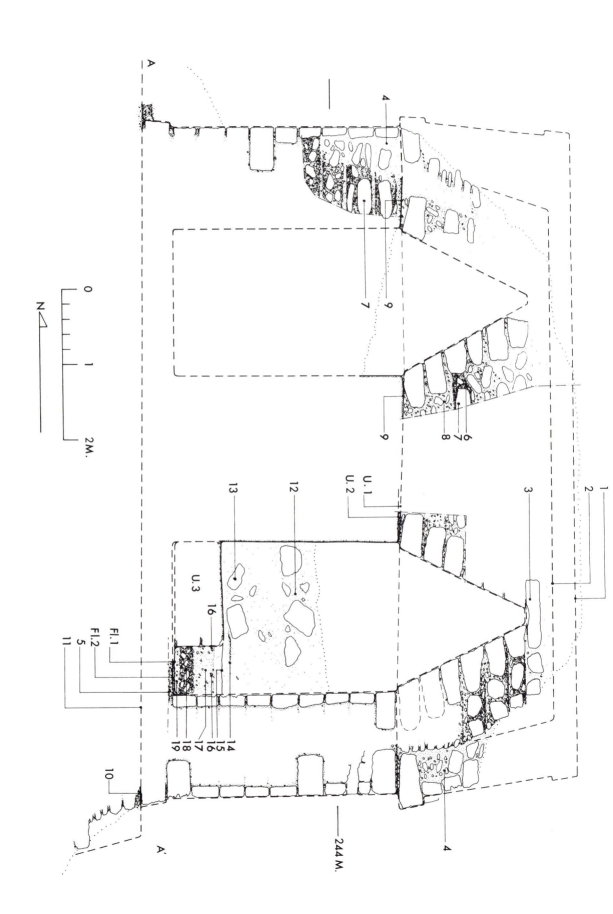

Figure 19. Structure 5E-1 Section/Profile A-A' 1:50. 1. estimated roof level. 2. assumed subroof. 3. preplastered capstone. 4. core mortar deteriorated. 5. mortar top of building platform. 6. dark mortar layer. 7. cushion-shaped core block. 8. light mortar layer. 9. plastered wall top. 10. top of supplementary platform. 11. assumed continuation of supplementary platform. 12. final collapse debris. 13. initial collapse debris. 14. ash layer. 15. top of unit 3 (off section). 16. corn cobs. 17. gray ashy layer, scattered sherds, and charcoal. 18. dark earth, ash, scattered sherds. 19. white powdery material, probably plaster debris.

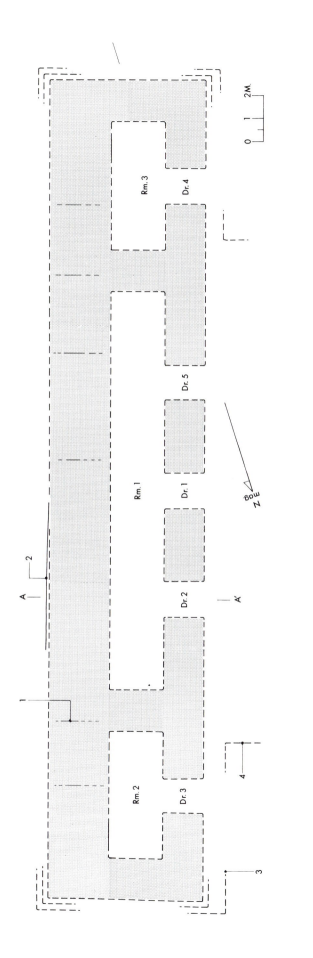

Figure 20. Structure 5C-9 Plan. Increase size 170% to achieve standard Tikal scale of 1:100. 1. line of task unit in wall core. 2. exterior wall facing displaced outward. 3. estimated top of lower substructure. 4. estimated location of stair side.

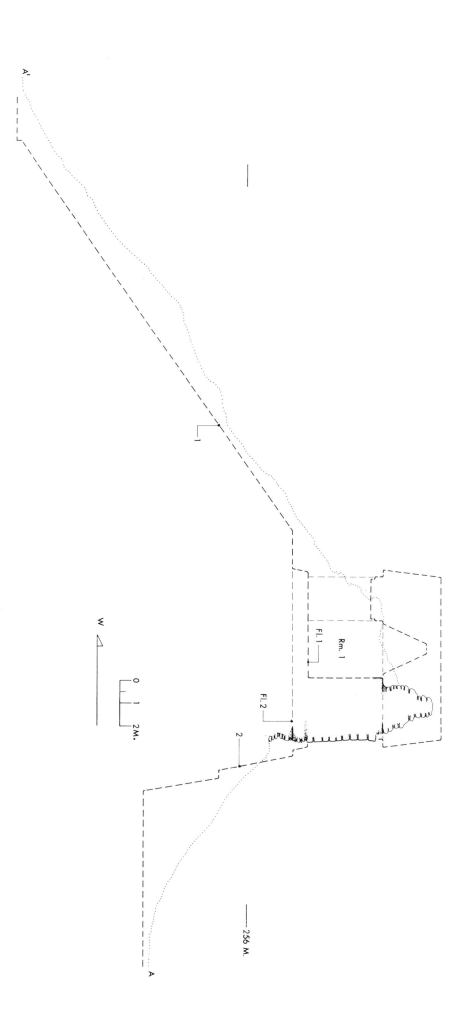

Figure 21. Structure 5C-9 Section/Profile A-A'. Increase size 170% to achieve standard Tikal scale of 1:100. 1. stair line. 2. rear terrace line.

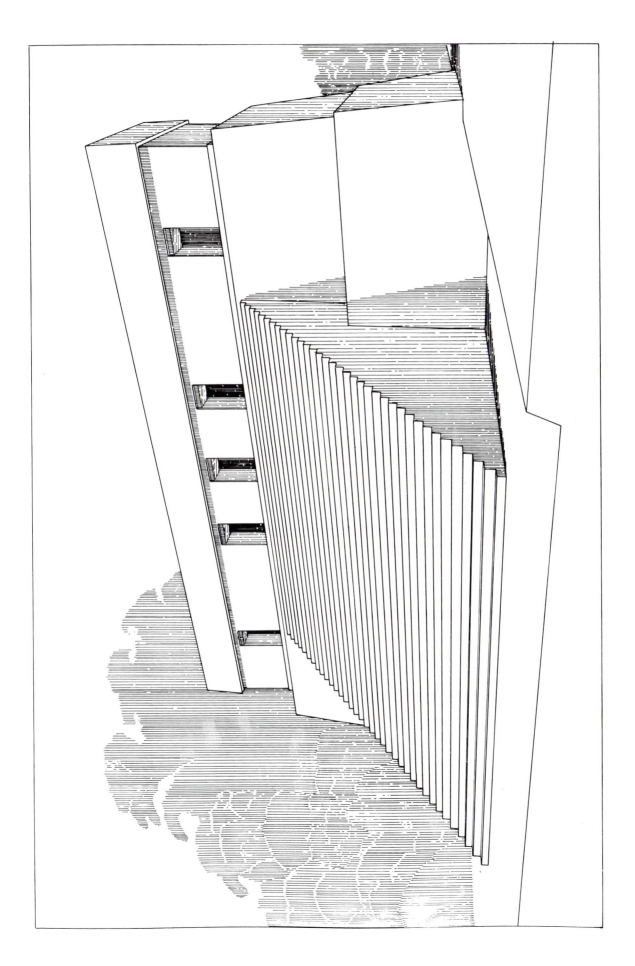

Figure 22. Structure 5C-9. Perspective Reconstruction.

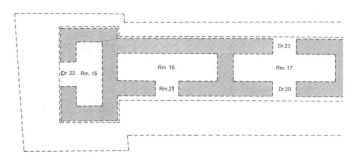

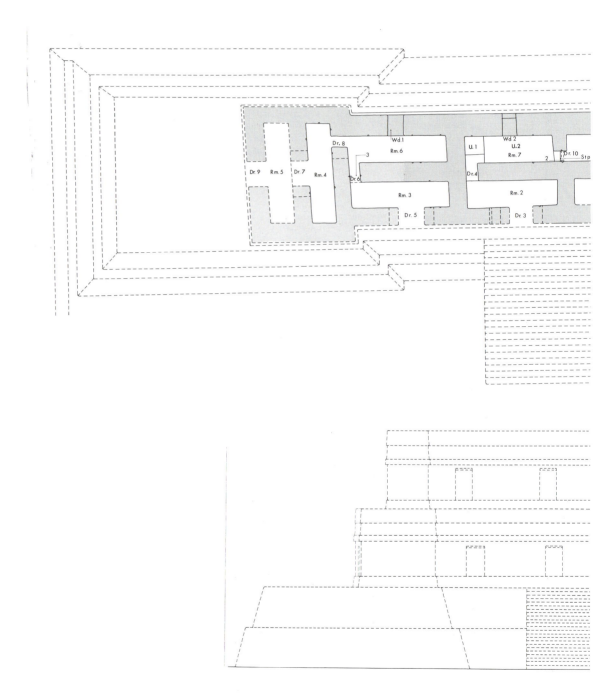

Figure 23. Structure 5C-13. a. Plan. Increase size 265% to achieve standard Tikal scale of 1:100. 1. subspring beam. 2. secondary doorway screen. 3. doorway jamb beam. 4. wall opening. b. Plan of Upper Story. Increase size 265% to achieve standard Tikal scale of 1:100. c. East Elevation. Increase size 373% to achieve standard Tikal scale of 1:100.

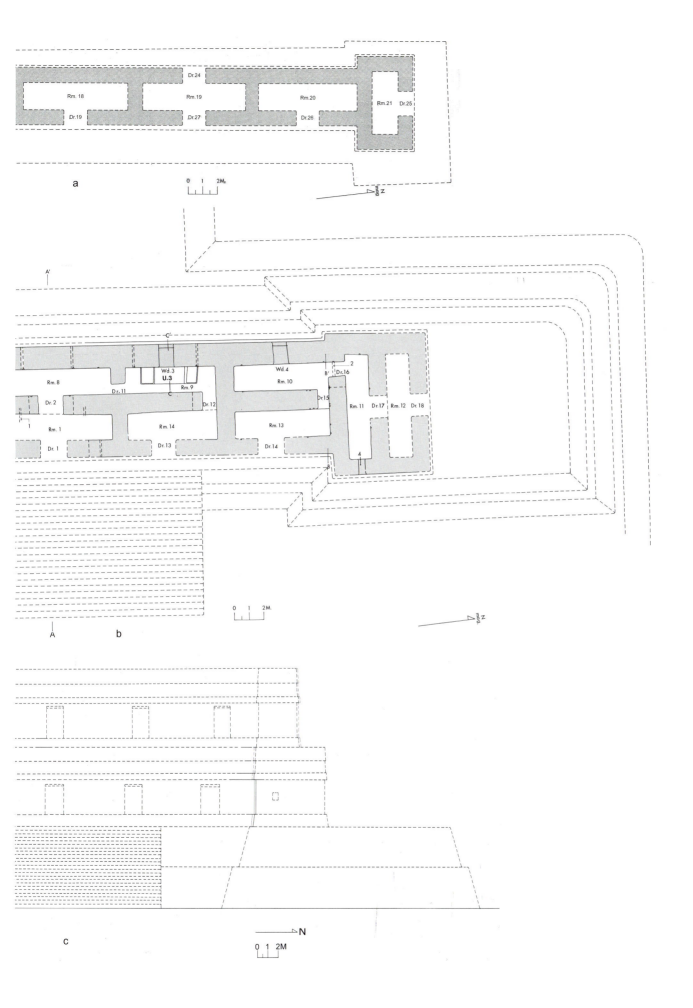

a

Rm. 18   Dr.24   Rm.19   Rm.20   Rm.21   Dr.25
Dr.19   Dr.27   Dr.26

0   1   2M.

N m.g.

A'

C'   Wd.3   Wd.4   2   Dr.16
Rm. 8   U.3   Rm. 9   Rm.10   B'   Dr.15   Rm. 11   Dr.17   Rm.12   Dr.18
Dr. 2   Dr. 11   Dr.12
Rm. 1   Rm. 14   Rm.13
Dr. 1   Dr.13   Dr.14   4

0   1   2M.

N m.g.

A   b

c

N

0 1   2M

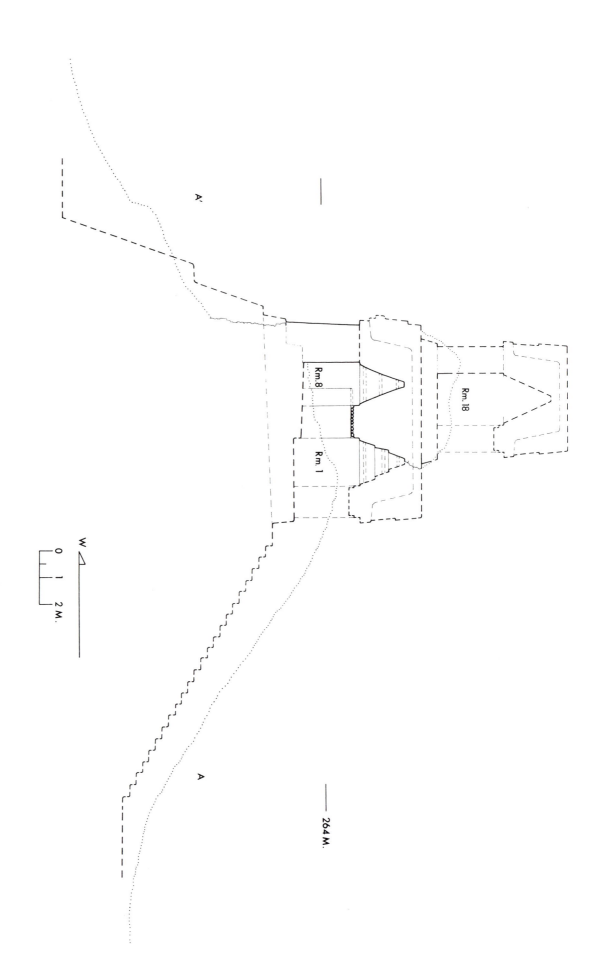

Figure 24. Structure 5C-13. Section/Profile A-A'. Increase size 145% to achieve standard Tikal scale of 1:100.

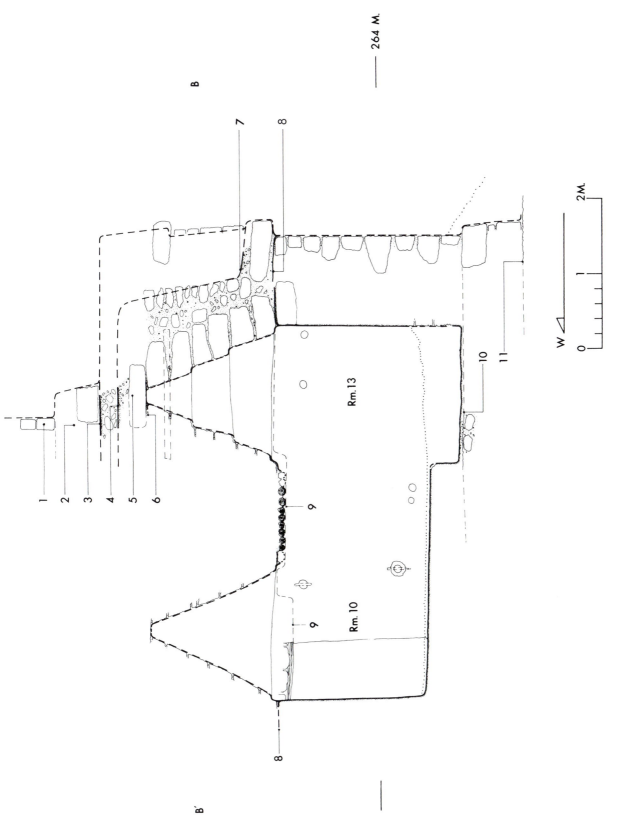

Figure 25. Structure 5C-13 Section/Profile B-B' 1:50. 1. exterior wall facing, upper story. 2. upper-story platform. 3. plastered roof of building. 4. plastered subroof. 5. preplastered capstone. 6. plaster turn of vault soffit. 7. hard, smooth plaster. 8. plastered wall top. 9. plastered lintel bed. 10. mortar top of building platform. 11. mortar top of supplementary platform.

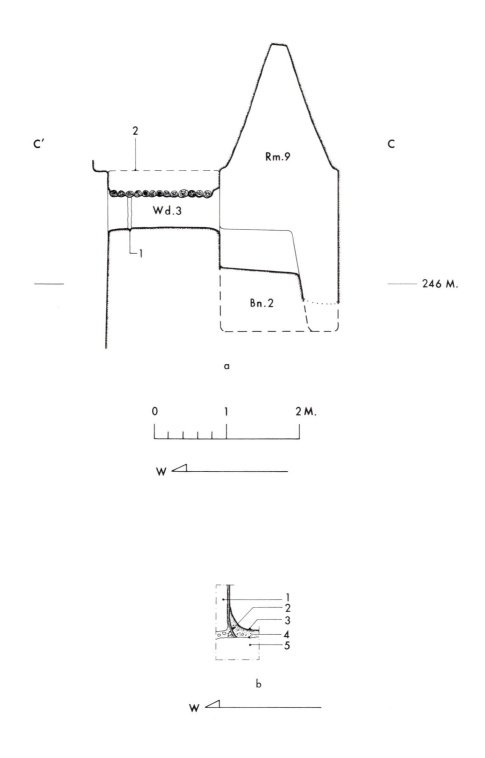

Figure 26. Structure 5C-13. a. Section/Profile C-C' 1:50. 1. groove in sill and jambs. 2. plastered wall top. b. Floor-wall Detail 1:50. 1. interior wall facing masonry. 2. wall plaster. 3. floor plaster. 4. mortar layer. 5. building platform core.

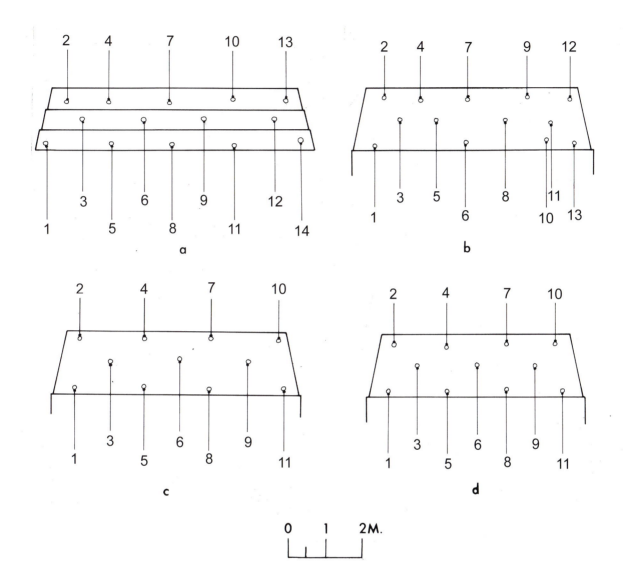

Figure 27. Structure 5C-13 Rear Vault Beam Patterns. a. Room 1. b. Room 4. c. Room 9. d. Room 7.

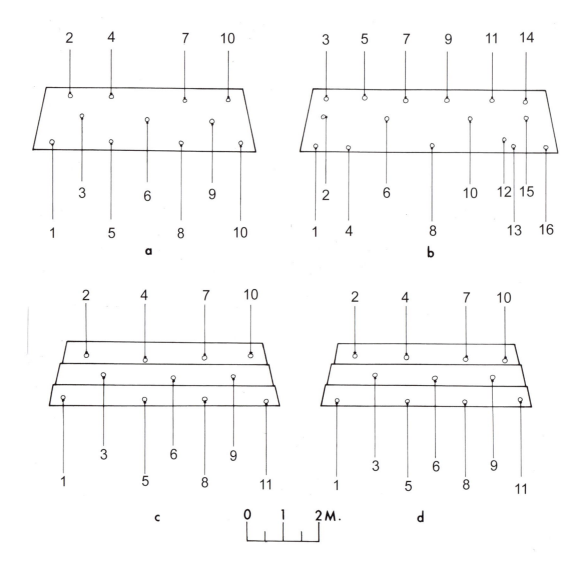

Figure 28. Structure 5C-13 Rear Vault Beam Patterns. a. Room 10. b. Room 11. c. Room 13. d. Room 14.

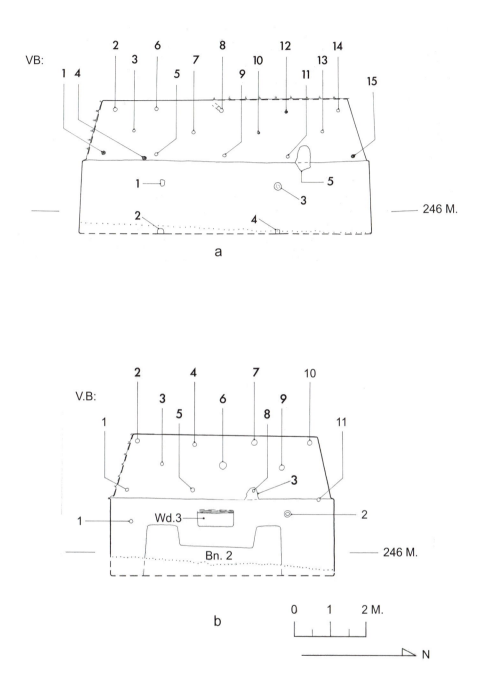

Figure 29. Structure 5C-13. a. West Elevation, Room 8 1:100. 1, 2, 3, 4. through-wall holes. 5. recent looter hole. b. West Elevation, Room 9 1:100. 1, 2. through-wall holes. 3. recent looter hole.

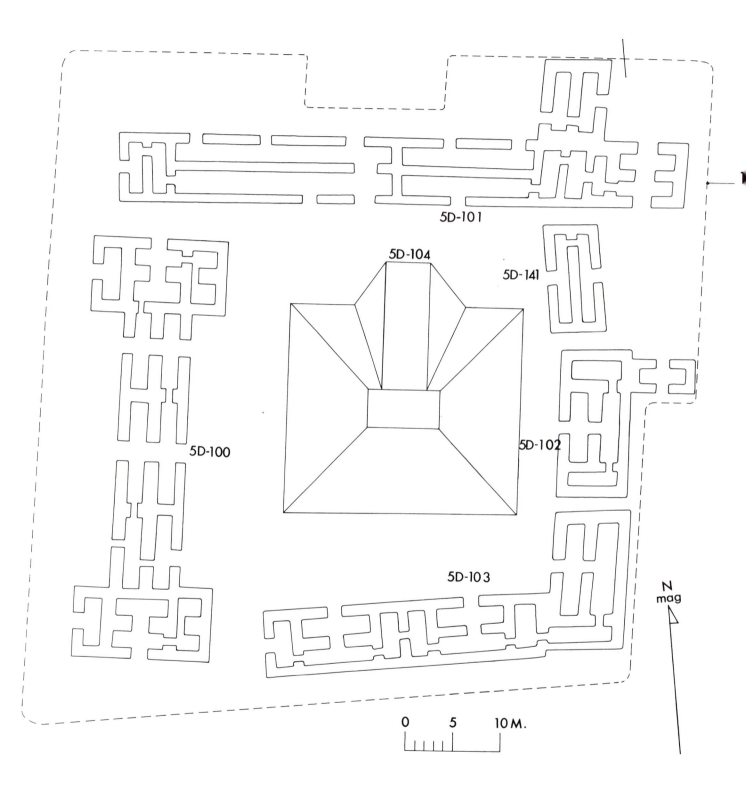

Figure 30. Group 5D-14 Plan 1:400. 1. approximate top of Platform 5D-30.

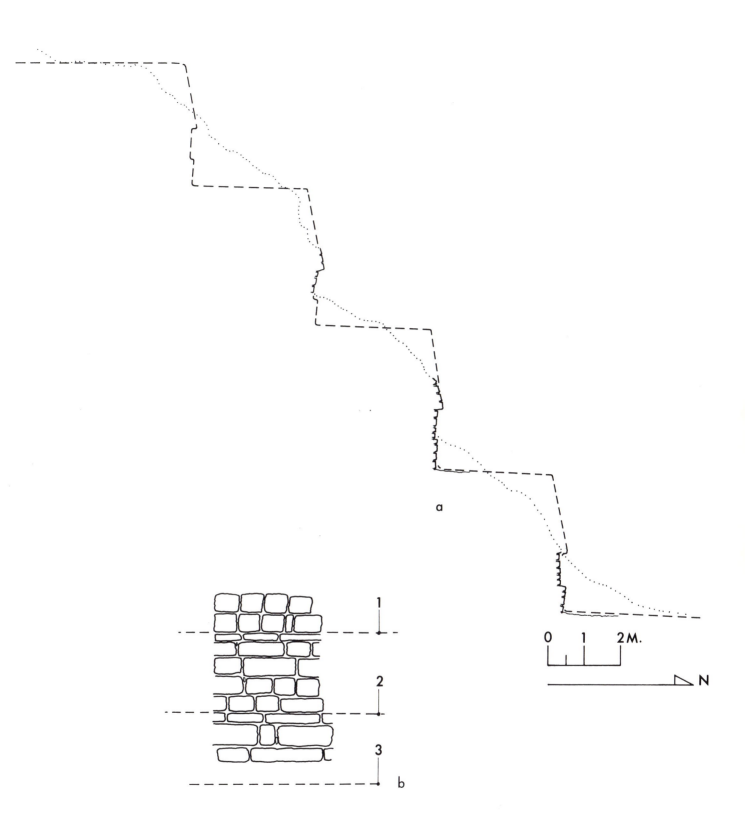

Figure 31. Group 5D-14. a. Terrace Profile 1:100. b. Elevation 1:50. 1. apron outset. 2. basal molding. 3. base level.

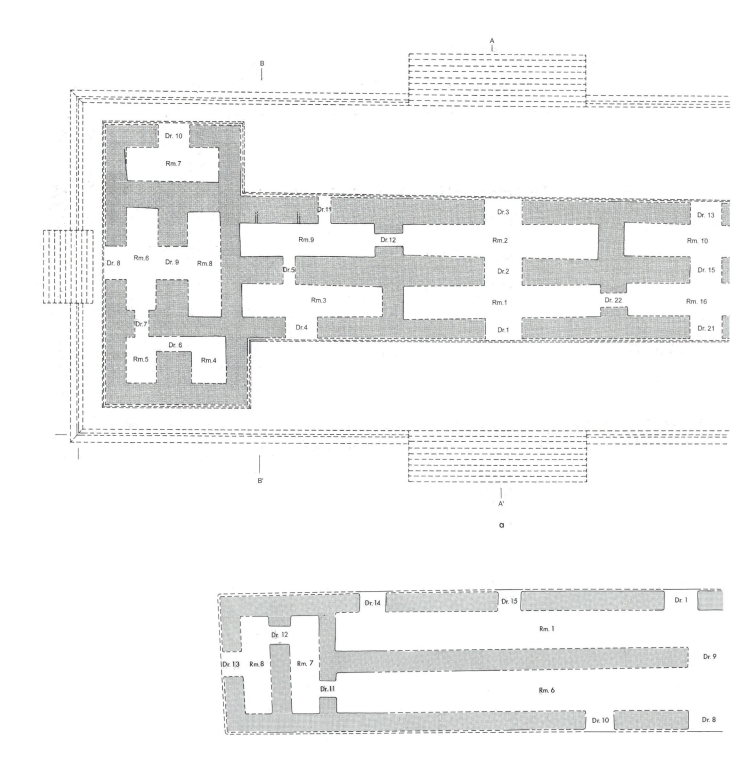

Figure 32. a. Structure 5D-100 Plan. Increase size 200% to achieve standard Tikal scale of 1:100. b. Structure 5D-101 and 5D-141 Plan 1. Increase size 200% to achieve standard Tikal scale of 1:100. 1. approximate top of Platform 5D-30.

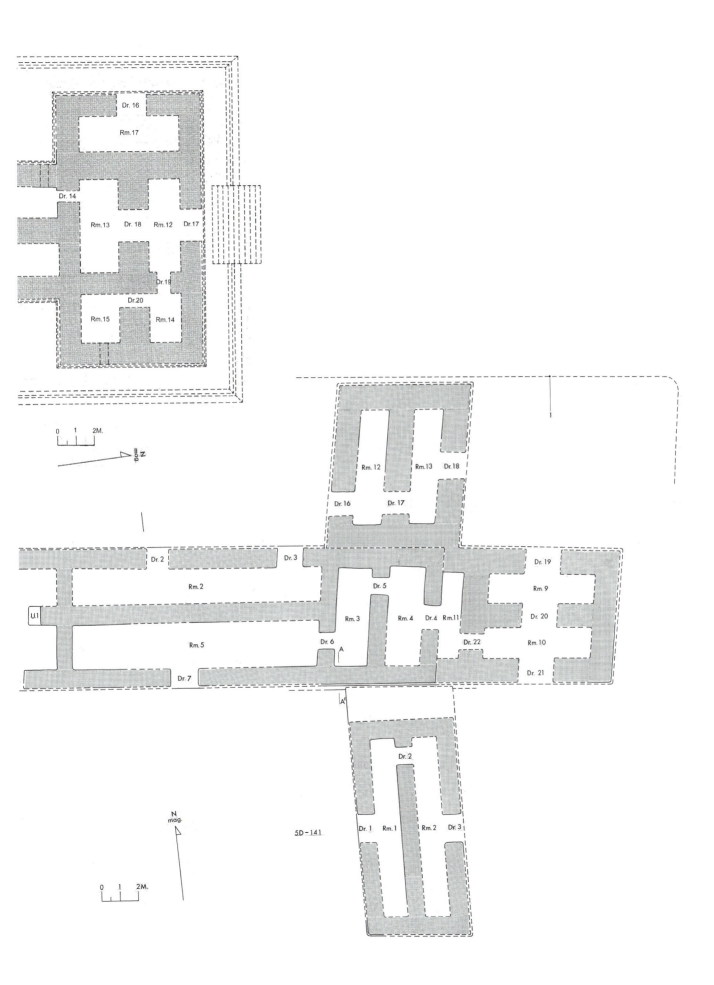

Dr. 16

Rm.17

Dr. 14

Rm.13 Dr. 18 Rm.12 Dr.17

Dr.19

Dr.20

Rm.15 Rm.14

0 1 2M.

N
mag.

Rm. 12 Rm.13 Dr.18

Dr. 16 Dr. 17

Dr. 2 Dr. 3 Dr. 19

Rm.2 Rm. 9

Dr. 5

U.1 Dr. 20

Rm. 3 Rm. 4 Dr. 4 Rm.11

Rm. 5 Dr. 6 A Dr. 22 Rm. 10

Dr. 7 Dr. 21

A'

Dr. 2

N
mag.

5D – 141

Dr. 1 Rm. 1 Rm. 2 Dr. 3

0 1 2M.

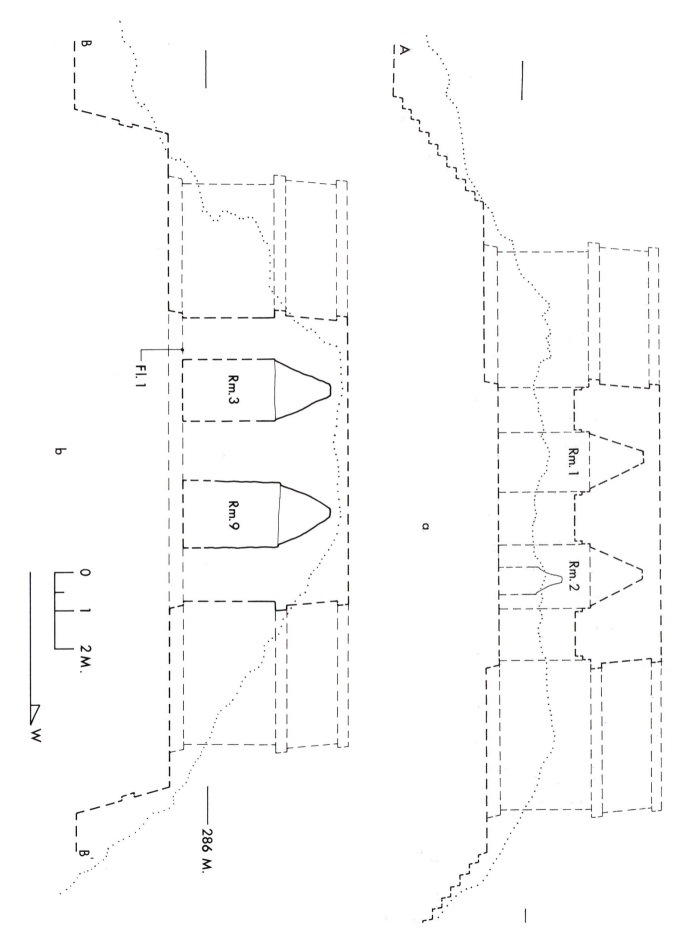

Figure 33. Structure 5D-100. a. Section/Profile A-A' 1:100. b. Section/Profile B-B' 1:100.

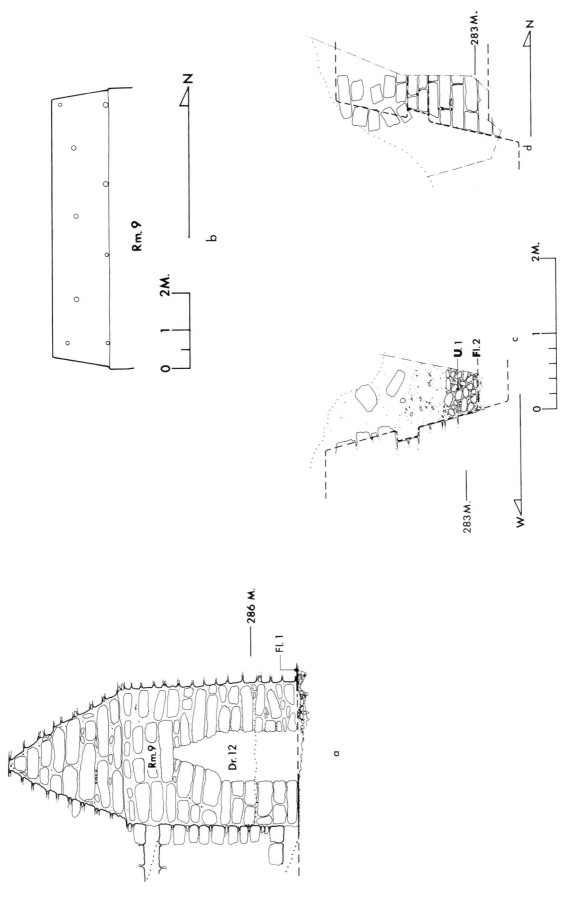

Figure 34. Structure 5D-100. a. Elevation Room 9 1:50. b. Vault Beam Pattern Room 9 1:100. c. Supplementary Platform Section 1:50. d. Supplementary Platform Elevation Detail 1:50.

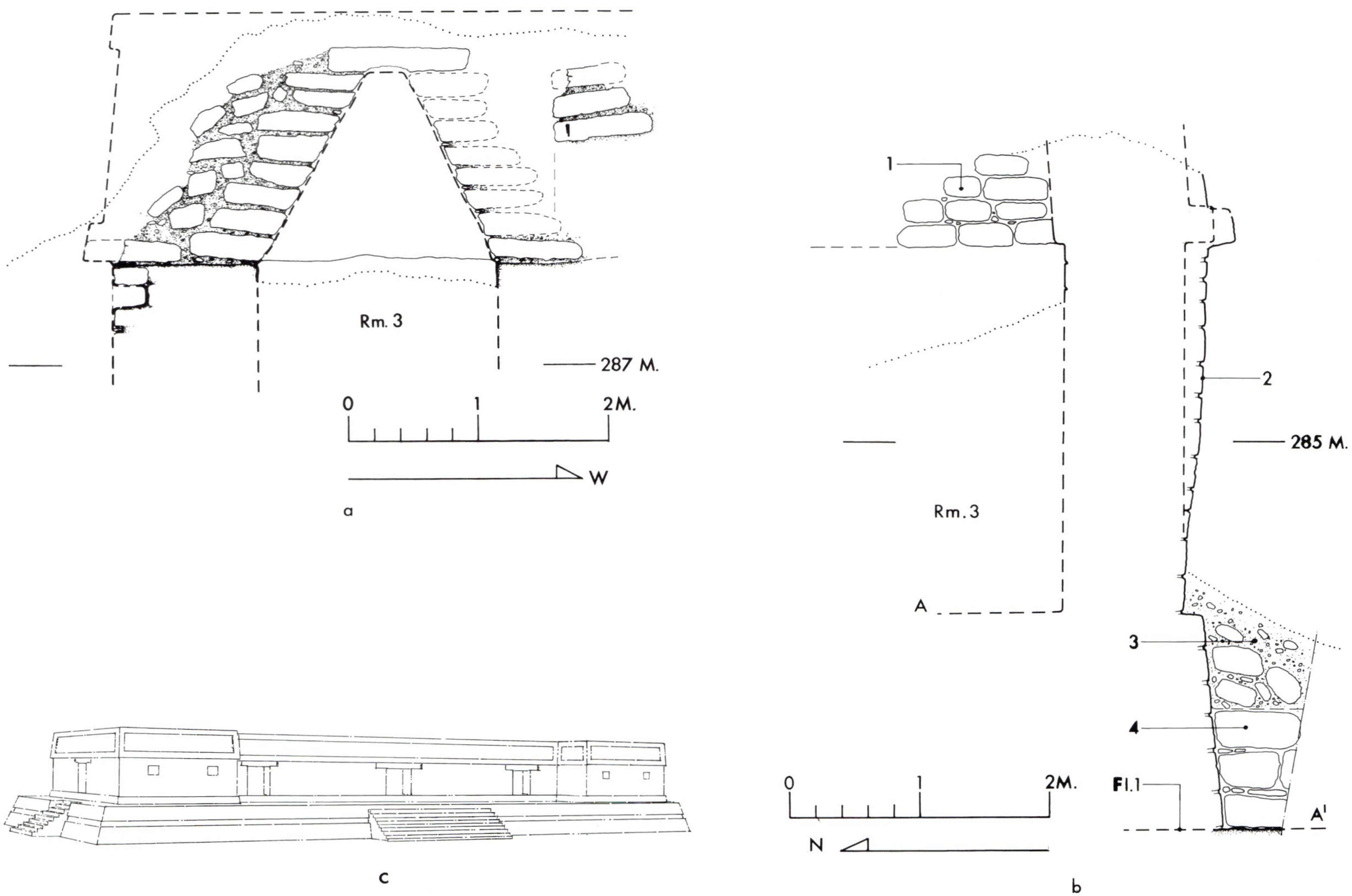

Figure 35. a. Structure 5D-100 Vault Section 1:50. 1. vault-back facing room 9. b. Structure 5D-101 Section/Profile A-A' 1:50. 1. vault stones in elevation. 2. wall line distorted outward. 3. collapse debris. 4. Structure 5D-141 substructure in elevation. c. Structure 5D-100 Perspective Reconstruction.

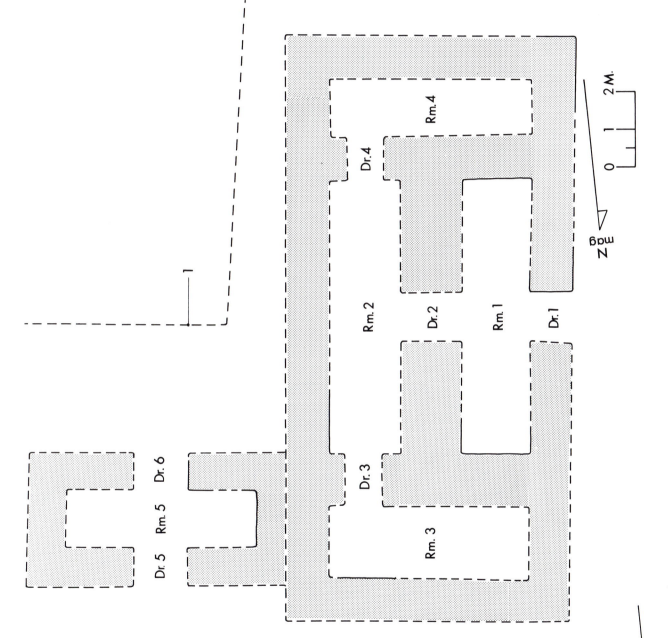

Figure 36. Structure 5D-102 Plan 1:100. 1. approximate top of Platform 5D-30.

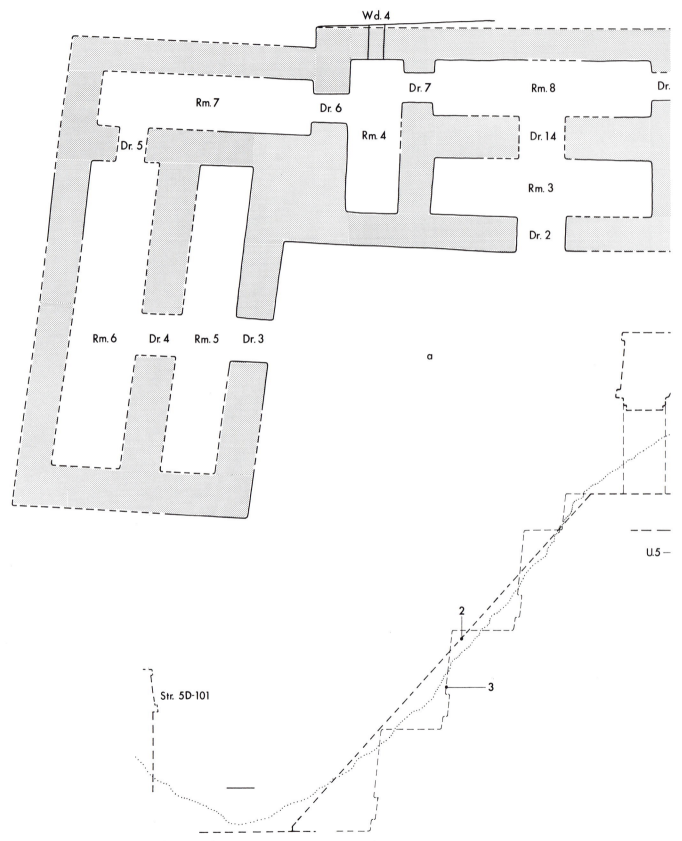

Figure 37. a. Structure 5D-103 Plan. Increase size 125% to achieve standard Tikal scale of 1:100. b. Structure 5D-104 Axial Section/Profile. Increase size 135% to achieve standard Tikal scale of 1:100. 1. estimated plaza floor. 2. estimated stair. 3. estimated location front terraces (off section).

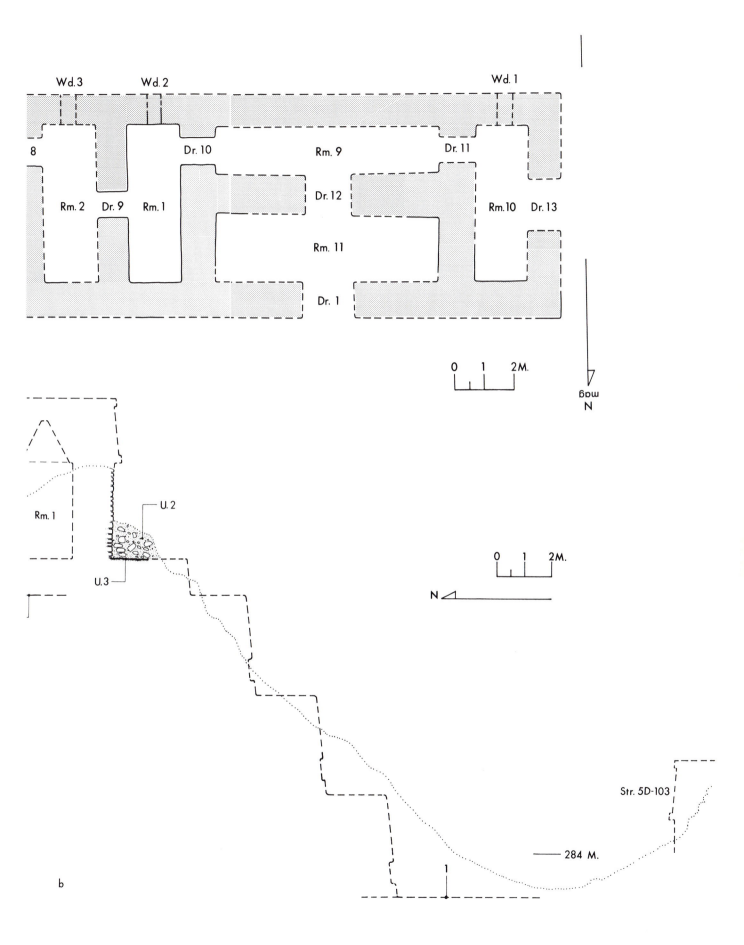

Wd. 3   Wd. 2   Wd. 1

8   Dr. 10   Rm. 9   Dr. 11

Rm. 2   Dr. 9   Rm. 1   Dr. 12   Rm. 10   Dr. 13

Rm. 11

Dr. 1

0   1   2 M.

mag
N

Rm. 1

U. 2

U. 3

0   1   2 M.

N

Str. 5D-103

284 M.

1

b

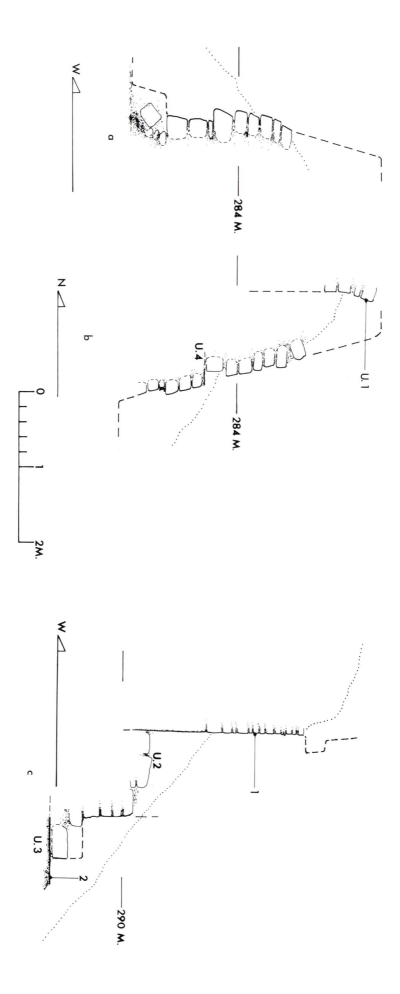

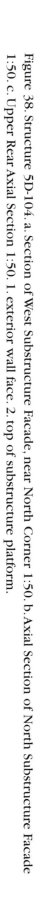

Figure 38. Structure 5D-104. a. Section of West Substructure Facade, near North Corner 1:50. b. Axial Section of North Substructure Facade 1:50. c. Upper Rear Axial Section 1:50. 1. exterior wall face. 2. top of substructure platform.

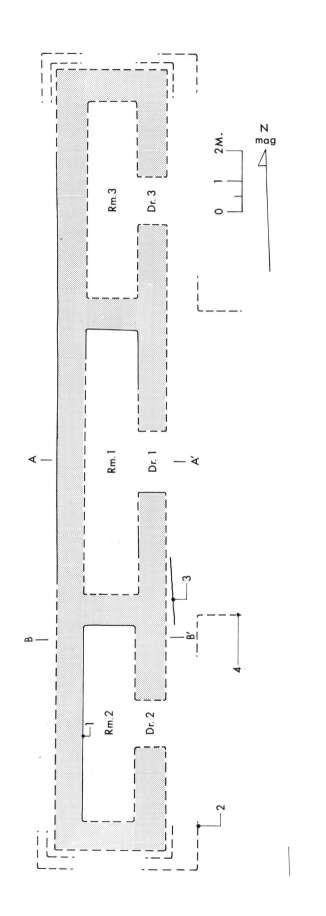

Figure 39. Structure 5D-105 Plan. Increase size 128% to achieve standard Tikal scale of 1:100. 1. interior wall line at wall-top level. 2. estimated top of lower substructure. 3. exterior wall face displaced outward. 4. estimated location of stair side.

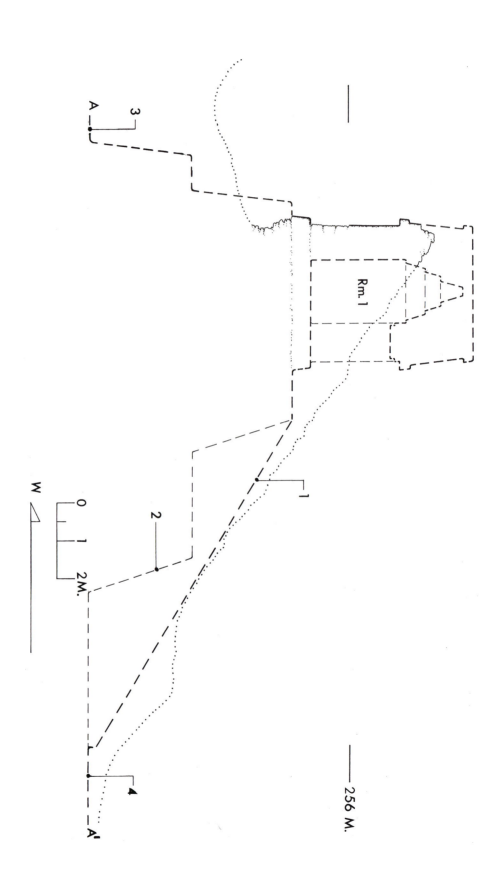

256 M.

Figure 40. Structure 5D-105 Section/Profile A-A' 1:100. 1. stair line. 2. front terrace off section. 3. base level. 4. estimated plaza floor level.

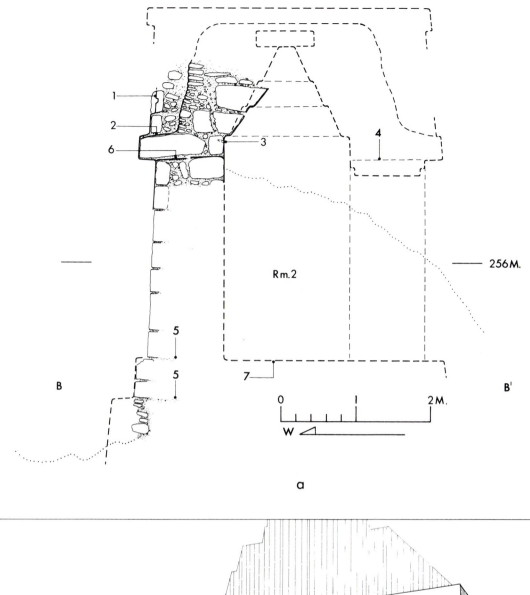

256M.

Rm.2

B

B'

0   1   2M.

W

a

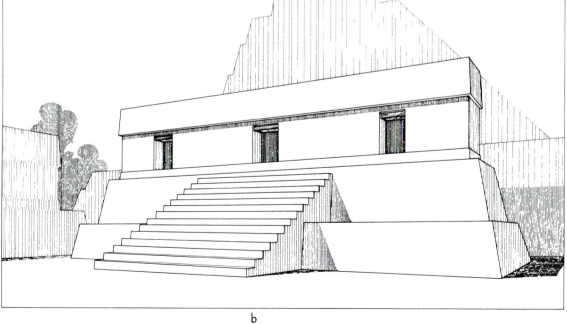

b

Figure 41. Structure 5D-105. a. Section/Profile B-B' 1:50. 1. carved upper zone. 2. hard plaster on medial corbel. 3. rod row hole, 0.03 diameter. 4. wall top, off section. 5. rough mortar level. 6. plastered wall top. 7. assumed floor level. b. Perspective Reconstruction.

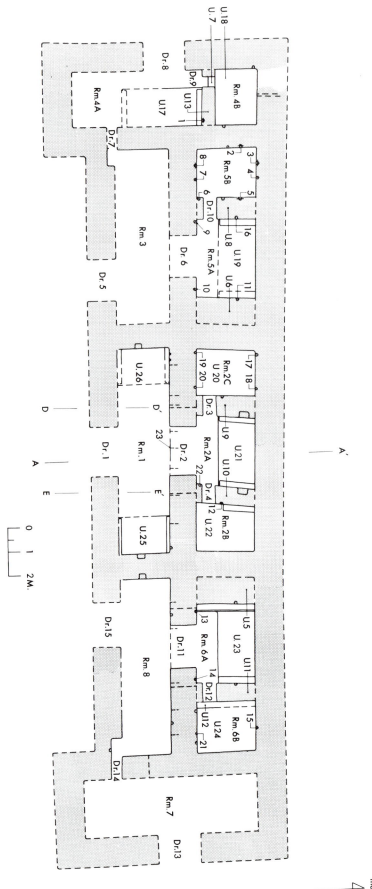

Figure 42. Structure 5E-51 Plan. Increase size 160% to achieve standard Tikal scale of 1:100. 1-22. cord holders. 23. rod row.

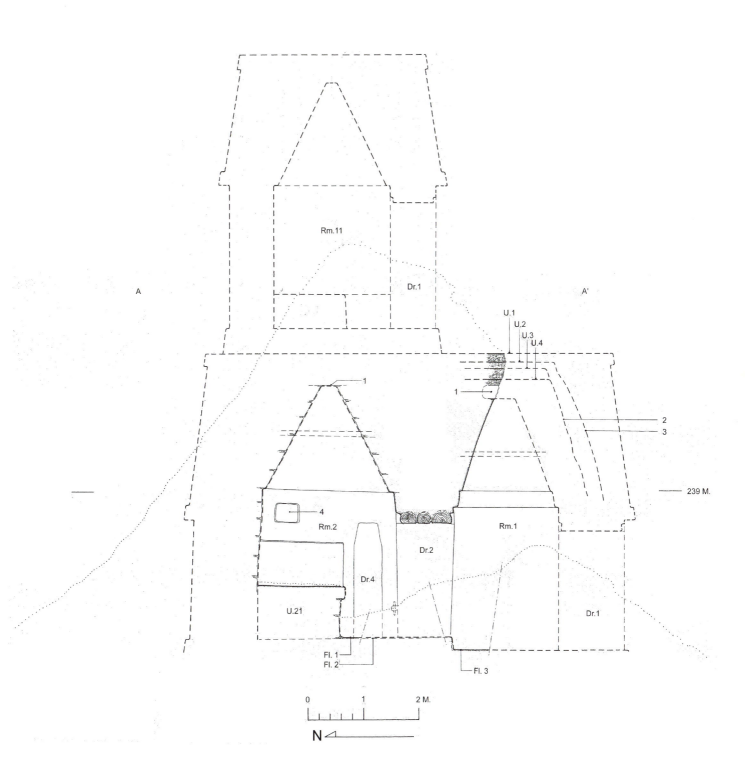

Figure 43. Structure 5E-51 Section/Profile A-A'. Increase size 150% to achieve standard Tikal scale of 1:50. 1. preplastered capstone. 2. preliminary vault back. 3. final vault back. 4. niche.

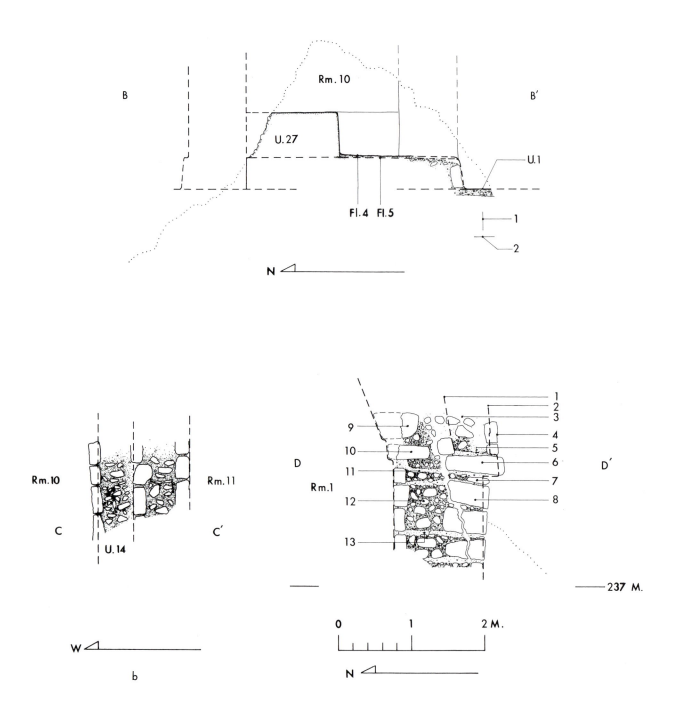

Figure 44. Structure 5E-51. a. Section/Profile B-B' 1:50. 1. front face of spine wall in building. 2. capstone soffit, room 1. b. Section/Profile C-C' 1:50. c. Section/Profile D-D' 1:50. 1. final vault back. 2. reconstructed line of upper-zone facing. 3. upper-zone core. 4. carved upper-zone facing stone. 5. mortar surface at foot of vault back. 6. medial corbel. 7. leveling course. 8. exterior wall facing header. 9. vault soffit header. 10. subspring corbel. 11. mortar wall top. 12. wall core. 13. white mortar course level.

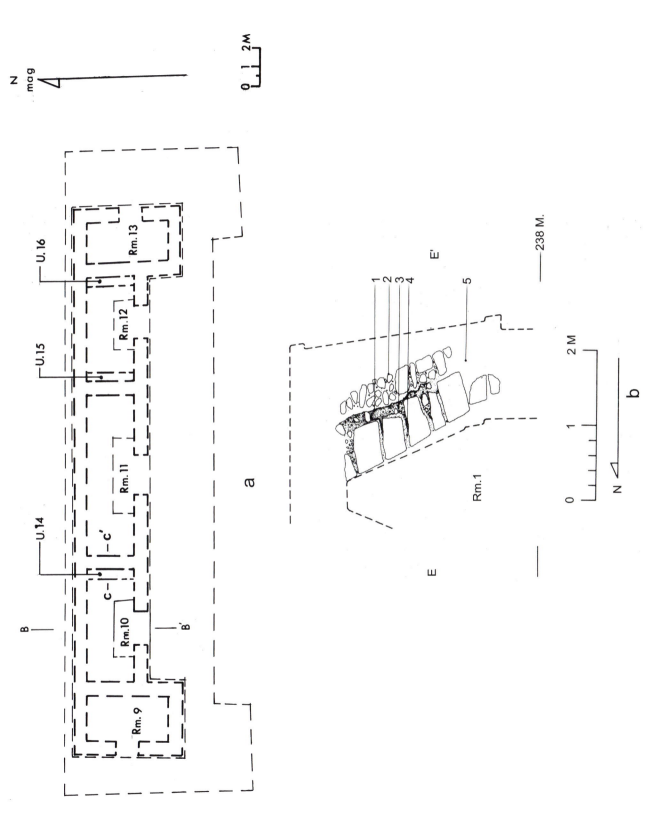

Figure 45. a. Structure 5E-51 Diagrammable Plan of Upper Story 1:200 (for orientation see Fig. 42). b. Section/Profile E-E' 1:50. 1. preliminary vault back. 2. final vault back. 3. gray mortar. 4. white mortar. 5. masonry displaced outward.

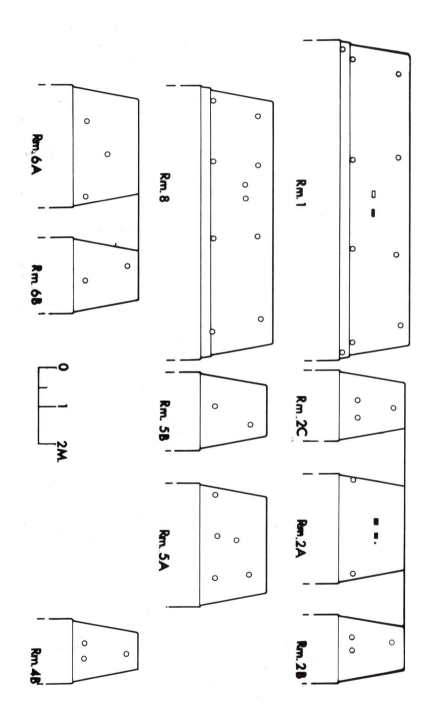

Figure 46. Structure 5E-51 Vault Beam Patterns 1:100.

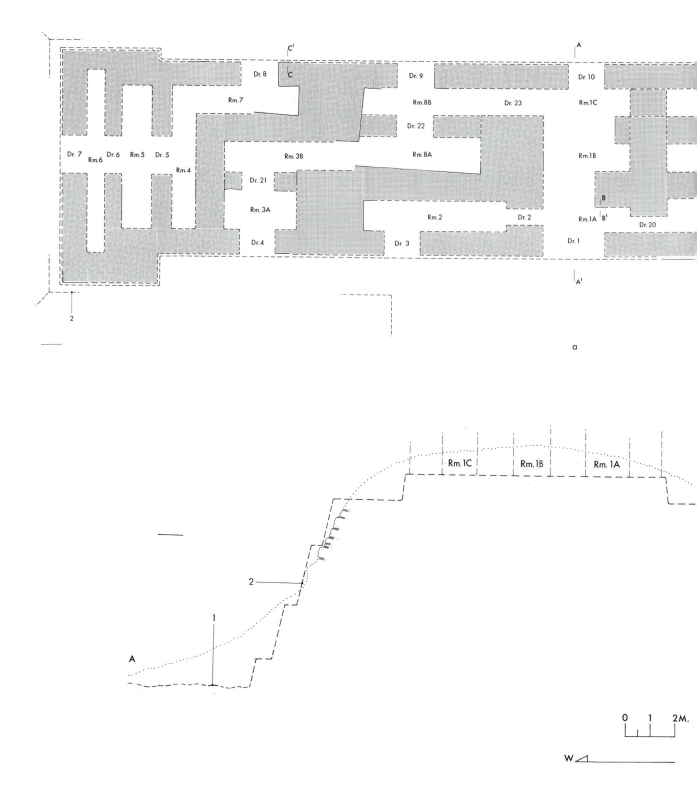

Figure 47. Structure 5E-55. a. Plan. Increase size 200% to achieve standard Tikal scale of 1:100. 1. approximate location of stair side. 2. approximate line of supplementary platform top. b. Section/Profile A-A'. Increase size 140% to achieve standard Tikal scale of 1:100. 1. natural grade. 2. rear terrace line. 3. front terrace line. 4. plaza floor level. 5. stair line.

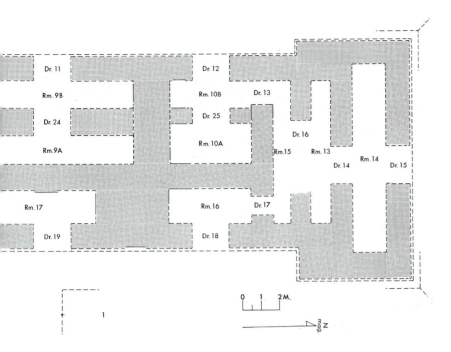

Dr. 11   Dr. 12
Rm. 9B   Rm. 10B   Dr. 13
Dr. 24   Dr. 25
Rm.9A   Rm.10A   Dr. 16
Rm.15   Rm. 13   Rm. 14
Dr. 14   Dr. 15
Rm.17   Rm.16   Dr. 17
Dr. 19   Dr. 18

1

0   1   2 M.

Z mag.

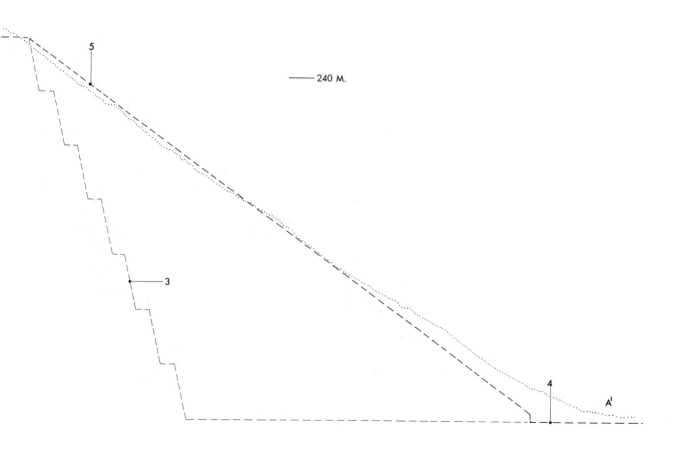

5

—— 240 M.

3

4   A¹

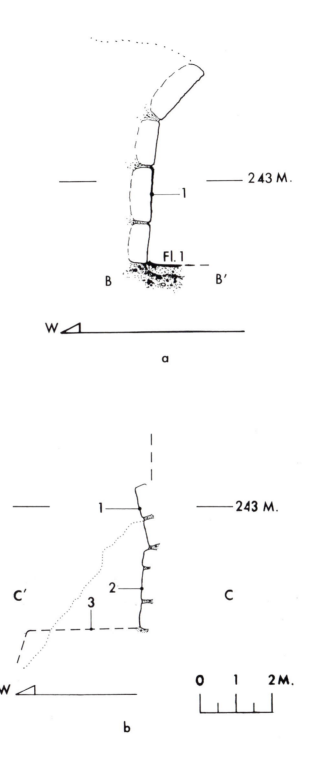

Figure 48. Structure 5E-55. a. Section/Profile B-B' 1:50. 1. interior wall facing. b. Section/Profile C-C' 1:50. 1. exterior wall facing. 2. facing of building platform. 3. top of supplementary platform.

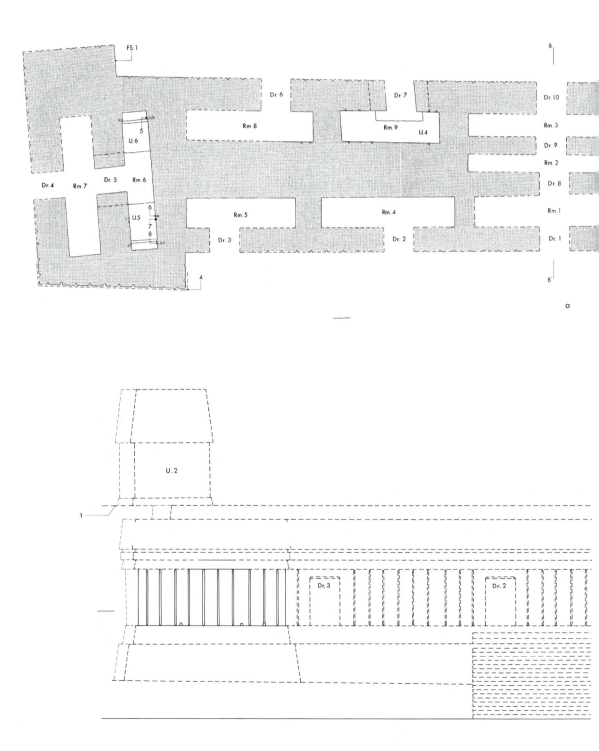

Figure 49. Structure 5E-58. a. Plan. Increase size 200% to achieve standard Tikal scale of 1:100. 1. discontinuity in wall line. 2. tunnel entrance. 3. tunnel exit. 4. building platform. 5-9. subspring beam holes. b. East Elevation. Increase size 208% to achieve standard Tikal scale of 1:100. 1. extension of upper-level roof. 2. tunnel entrance.

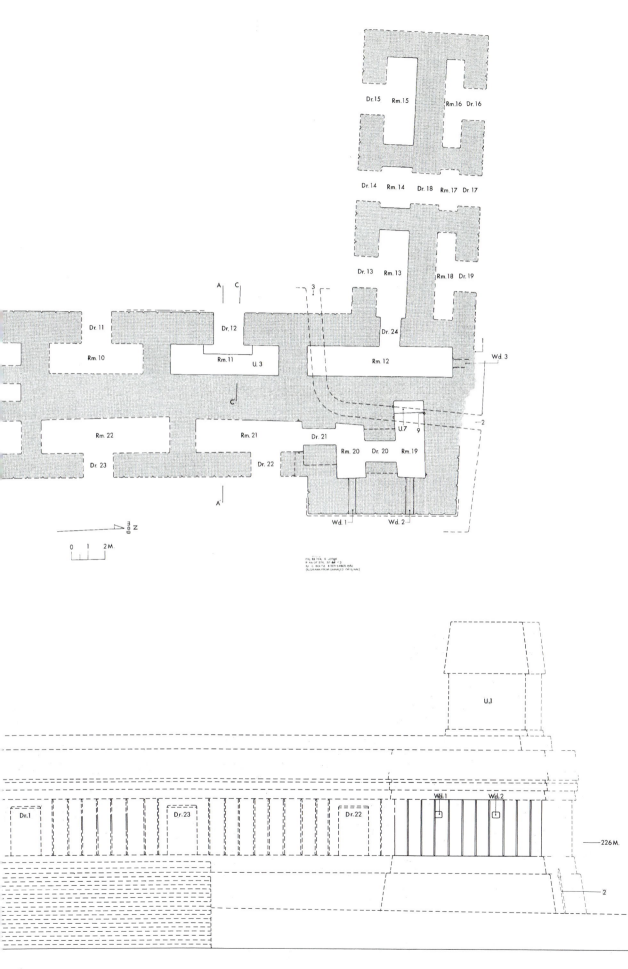

Dr.15　Rm.15　　　　Rm.16 Dr.16

Dr.14　Rm.14　Dr.18　Rm.17　Dr.17

Dr.13　Rm.13　　Rm.18　Dr.19

A C　　3

Dr.11　Dr.12　Dr.24　　Wd.3

Rm.10　Rm.11　U.3　Rm.12

C　　　2

U.7　9

Rm.22　Rm.21　Dr.21　Rm.20　Dr.20　Rm.19

Dr.23　Dr.22

A'

Wd.1　Wd.2

N
mag

0　1　2 M.

U.1

Dr.1　Dr.23　Dr.22　Wd.1　Wd.2

226 M.

2

b

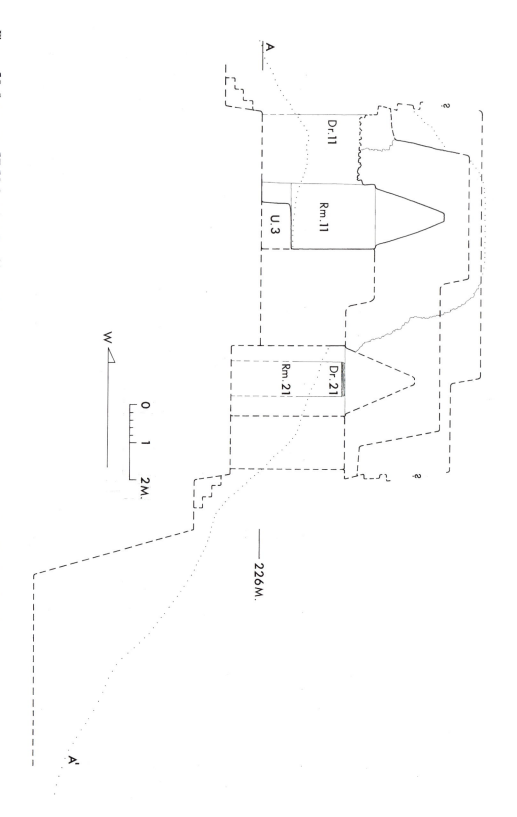

Figure 50. Structure 5E-58 Section/Profile A-A'. Increase size 200% to achieve standard Tikal scale of 1:100.

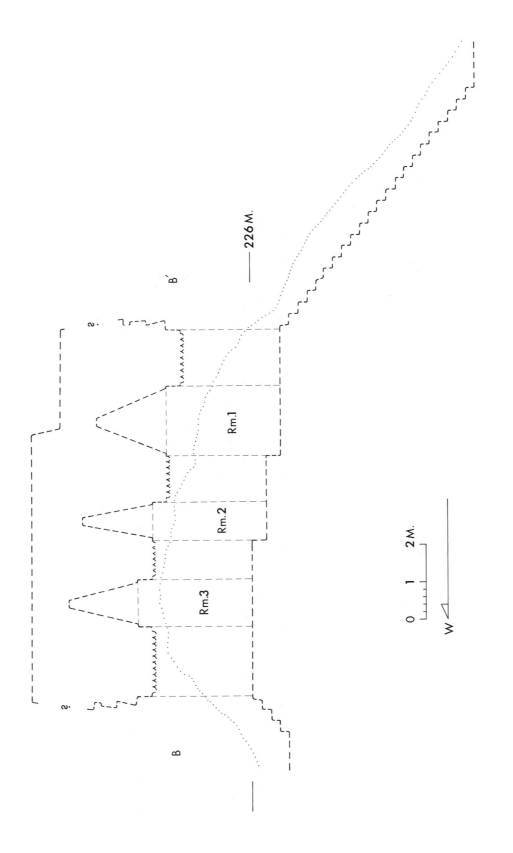

B'

—— 226 M.

Rm.1

Rm.2

Rm.3

B

W

0   1   2 M.

Figure 51. Structure 5E-58 Section/Profile B-B' 1:100.

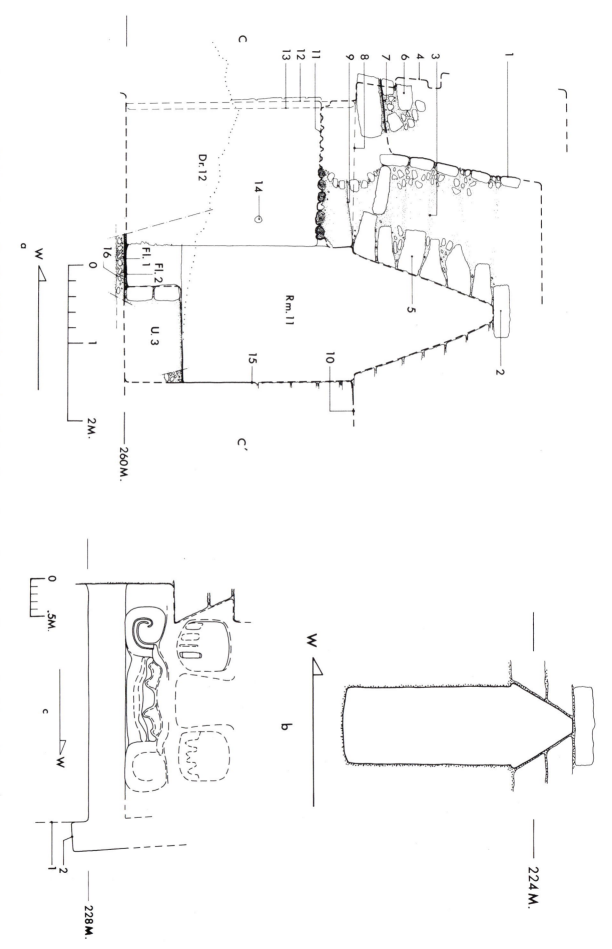

Figure 52. Structure 5E-58. a. Section/Profile C-C' 1:50. 1. vault-back facing. 2. preplastered capstone. 3. course level in vault core. 4. upper-zone profile. 5. vault-soffit headers. 6. butt of corbel course. 7. hard plaster 8. plastered wall top (off section). 9. top of supra-lintel masonry. 10. plastered wall top. 11. assumed lintel beams. 12. reconstructed wall face. 13. vertical groove. 14. jamb hole. 15. interior wall plaster. 16. top of building platform. b. Tunnel Profile 1:50. c. Facade Sculpture 1 1:50. 1. abutment with Structure 5E-57. 2. underside of medial molding.

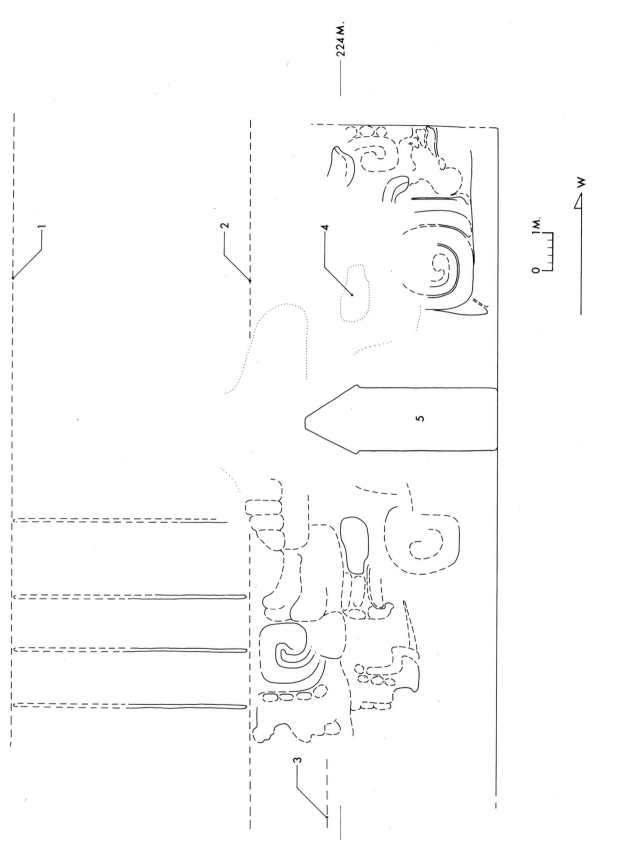

Figure 53. Structure 5E-58 Facade Sculpture 2 1:50. 1. underside of medial molding. 2. top of building platform. 3. top of supplementary platform. 4. left eye of principal motif. 5. tunnel entrance.

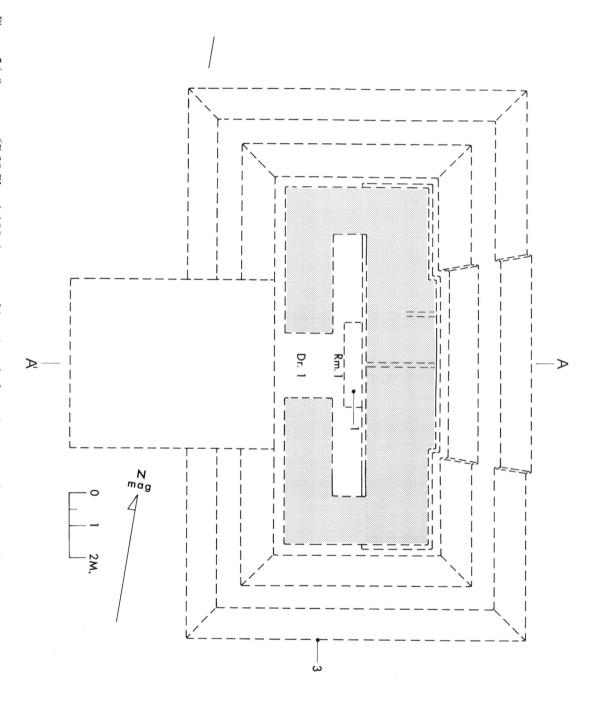

Figure 54. Structure 6B-30 Plan 1:100. 1. assumed interior platform. 2. estimated group platform edge. 3. estimated base line.

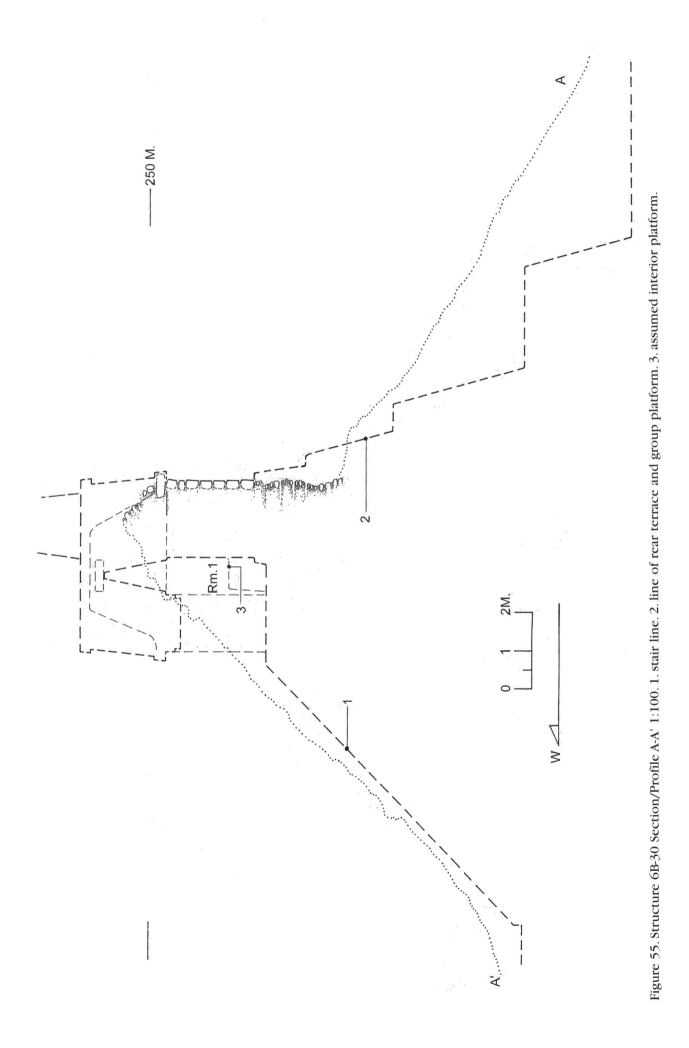

Figure 55. Structure 6B-30 Section/Profile A-A' 1:100. 1. stair line. 2. line of rear terrace and group platform. 3. assumed interior platform.

Figure 56. Structure 6B-30 Perspective Reconstruction.

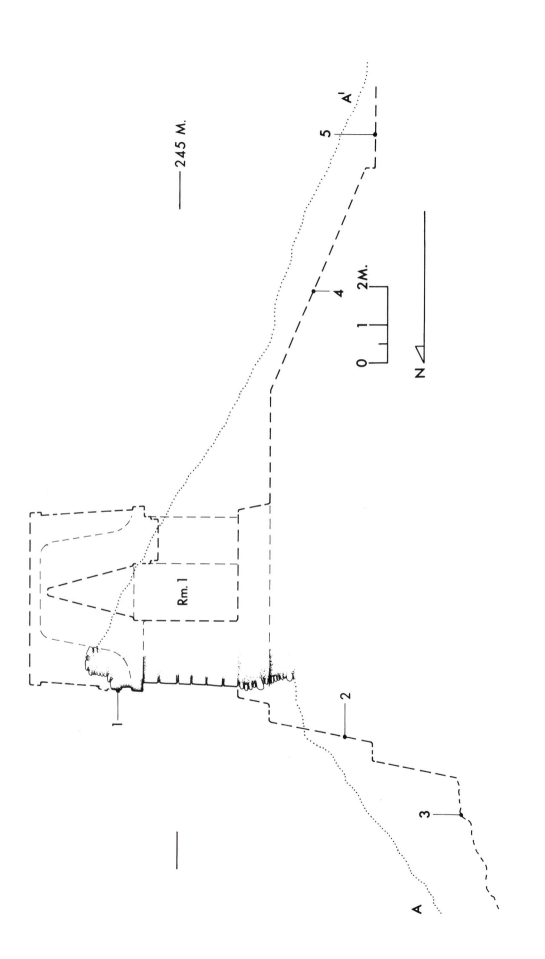

Figure 57. Structure 6B-33 Section/Profile A-A' 1:100. 1. upper-zone sculpture. 2. rear terrace line. 3. natural grade. 4. stair line. 5. plaza floor level.

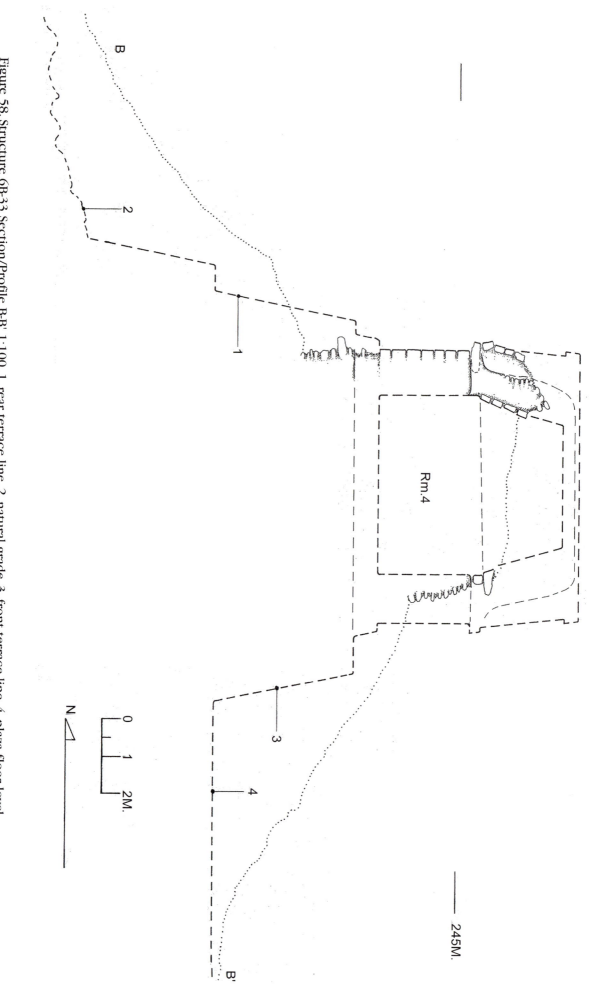

Figure 58. Structure 6B-33 Section/Profile B-B' 1:100. 1. rear terrace line. 2. natural grade. 3. front terrace line. 4. plaza floor level.

Rm 4

B

B'

2

1

3

4

Rm 4

N

0
1
2M.

245M.

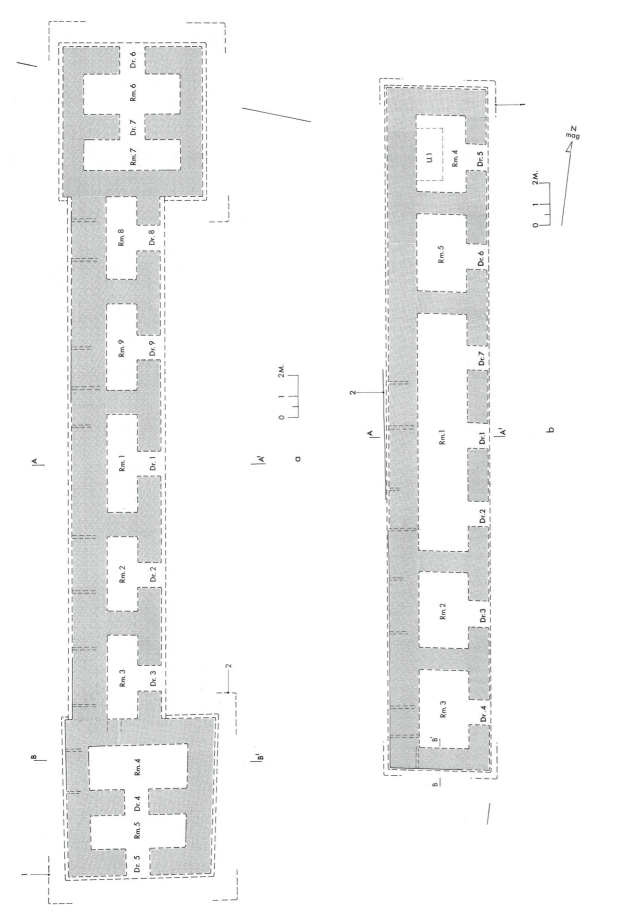

Figure 59. a. Structure 6B-33. Plan. Increase size 188% to achieve standard Tikal scale of 1:100. 1. estimated top of supplementary platform. 2. estimated location of stair side. b. Structure 6B-36 Plan. Increase size 188% to achieve standard Tikal scale of 1:100. 1. estimated top supplementary platform. 2. rear exterior wall face displaced outward.

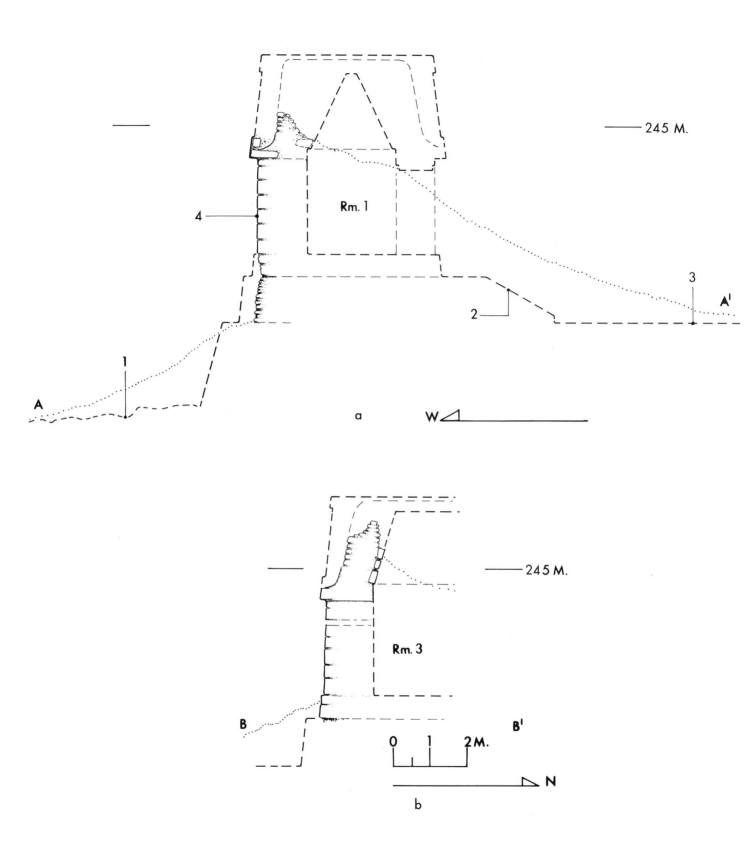

Figure 60. Structure 6B-36. a. Section/Profile A-A' 1:100. 1. natural grade. 2. stair line. 3. plaza floor level. 4. rectified rear wall face. b. Section/Profile B-B' 1:100.

a.

b.

c.

d.

Figure 61. a. Structure 4D-14 Room 10 Vault Looking North. b. Structure 4D-14 Rear Facade Looking East. c. Structure 4E-47 North Wall of Building. d. Structure 4E-47 South Facade, East Lateral Side Extension.

a.

b.

c.

d.

Figure 62. Structure 4E-47 a. East Lateral Side Extension, Looking East. b. Window 2, Room 9. c. Doorway 9, Room 10. d. Window 2, Room 2.

a.

b.

c.

d.

Figure 63. a. Structure 4E-47 Vault, Room 9. b. Structure 4E-47 Exterior Wall Facing. c. Structure 5C-13 North Lateral Side Extension Rear Fascade, Looking North. d. Structure 5C-13 Vault and Upper Zone Looking North.

a.

b.

c.

d.

Figure 64. a. Structure 5E-1 Room 9 Looking West. b. Structure 5E-1 Graffito on North End Wall, Room 9. c. Structure 5C-13 Vault and Upper Zone at Line B-B' Front Facade, Looking North. d. Structure 5C-13 North Lateral Side Extension Rear Facade, Looking North.

a.

b.

c.

d.

Figure 65. a. Structure 5C-13 Upper-Zone Sculpture Rear Facade, Looking East. b. Structure 5C-13 Vault in First Range Looking North. c. Structure 5C-13 Exterior Wall Facing Masonry. d. Structure 5D-100 Building Platform.

a.   b.

c.

d.

Figure 66. Structure 5D-100. a. Building Platform. b. Supplementary Platform. c. Wall Holes in Room 9, West End. d. Wall Holes in Room 8, East End.

b.

a.

c.

d.

Figure 67. a. Structure 5D-100 Doorway 14. b. Structure 5D-100 Vault in Room 3. c. Structure 5E-51 Doorway 14 Looking North. d. Squared Vault Beams Room 1, Looking North.

a.

b.

c.

d.

Figure 68. Structure 5E-51. a. Doorway 14 Looking North. b. Squared Vault Beams Room 1, Looking North. c. Primary Cord Holder Vertical Peg. d. Primary Cord Holder Horizontal Bone Peg.

a.

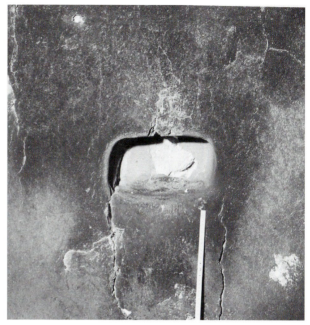

b.

c.

d.

Figure 69. a. Structure 5E-51 Cord Holder with Ceramic Insert. b. Structure 5E-51 Primary Niche. c. Structure 5E-51 Primary Niche. d. Structure 5E-58 North Facade.

a.

b.

c.

d.

Figure 70. Structure 5E-58. a. West Facade of Axial Wing Looking South. b. West Facade of Axial Wing Looking North. c. Southeast Corner of Courtyard Facade Sculpture 1 Visible at Center. d. Facade Sculpture 1.

a.

b.

c.

d.

Figure 71. Structure 5E-58. a. East Facade, South Lateral Side Extension Looking Southwest. b. East Facade, South Lateral Side Extension Looking Northwest; Building Platform and Core Masonry of Supplementary Platform. c. Doorway 21. d. East End of Room 6.

a.

b.

c.

d.

Figure 72. Structure 5E-58. a. Double Vault Mass between Rooms 19 and 20 Course Levels Visible in Core Masonry. b. Vaults, Room 11 Looking North. c. Miscellaneous Wall Hole, Room 11 Beam Removal Scars Visible. d. Doorway 11.

Index